On living and dying in West Texas:
A postmodern scrapbook

Jim W. Corder

on living and dying in
West Texas

A postmodern scrapbook

preface by
James S. Baumlin

introduction by
James S. Baumlin and Eric Knickerbocker

Moon City Press

Copyright © 2008 Moon City Press

Library of Congress Cataloging-in-Publication Data

Corder, Jim W. (Jim Wayne), 1929-
  A postmodern scrapbook : Jim W. Corder on living and dying in West Texas / edited by James S. Baumlin and Eric Knickerbocker.
     p. cm.
  ISBN-13: 978-0-913785-06-5 (pbk.)
  ISBN-10: 0-913785-06-7 (pbk.)
  1. Corder, Jim W. (Jim Wayne), 1929- 2. Corder, Jim W. (Jim Wayne), 1929—Childhood and youth. 3. Corder, Jim W. (Jim Wayne), 1929—Family. 4. Corder, Jim W. (Jim Wayne), 1929—Philosophy. 5. Aging–Philosophy. 6. Teachers–Texas–Biography. 7. Authors, American–20th century–Biography. 8. American poetry. 9. Texas, West–Social life and customs. 10. Texas, West–Biography. I. Baumlin, James S. II. Knickerbocker, Eric. III. Title.
  CT275.C7813A3 2008b
  976.4'063092–dc22
  [B]
                                    2007048132

Printed in the United States of America

CONTENTS

For Roberta and Sandra

Preface

I miss our walks greatly. I knew, every minute of the time, how happy I was to be with youenz. We move on-yes, we move on. But there was a kind of lovely poignancy in our aging friendship there. It's not the sort of thing that could be reclaimed. If we tried it again, it would probably be as Marx says about the difference between tragedy and farce. It's gone beyond recovery (except that, in my memory, I recover it again and again).

I am so grateful, not just to youenz, but to the nature of things, that I can carry away with me the sense of our truly humane relationship in that interim. Thanks. K. B.

So writes Kenneth Burke to his famous friend, Malcolm Cowley. I remember writing something to Jim W. Corder much less eloquent though no less grateful in sentiment, writing it some years after I had moved from Fort Worth and Texas Christian University (where I had taught in the English Department with Jim), writing it to Jim while he was undergoing chemotherapy for his first bout with cancer. Our walks, though, were quick: across campus to a local café, where cheap white wine and a quiet table held us for hours in the afternoon as we theorized together, penciling our grand notions upon the backs of paper napkins. Some of our theorizings—about teaching and writing, mainly—saw their way into print and we were both a little proud of them, I perhaps a little more so, being the junior professor.

"Yes, we move on," Burke writes. Yet it shocked me that afternoon when I was sitting in Jim's home attic-office, having gone with another colleague, a one-time student of Jim's, to retrieve unpublished manuscripts. Losing his second bout, Jim had recently passed away. Searching for manuscripts—Jim had left many, scattered throughout his home and school office—my letter surfaced out of a desk drawer. He never, to my knowledge, threw anything away: I imagine that somewhere, perhaps in a box or drawer I have not looked into, sit the napkins of our theorizing. And here Jim had kept the letter, having read it after puking (as he told me) from chemo. Sitting at the desk of the one addressed, how does one read one's own letter? How can one avoid impersonation, pretending a response? (But does it—the letter, the writing—remain one's own? Does one remain the same person who wrote, having since "moved on"?) It being a private missive, I would not want it read by others. Yet it is out of the same well of gratitude that this present manuscript comes into print; by its means I can thank Jim more formally, more publicly (if belatedly) for "our truly humane relationship in that interim."

Internal references suggest that *Scrapbook* is the last of Jim's several remaining, unpublished book manuscripts. Though he had much left in him to write, he simply ran out of time. While his published writings reached ever-widening circles of scholars and general readers, my co-editor and I offer *Scrapbook* primarily to that more intimate circle of Jim's friends, students, colleagues—in brief, to his most avid readers, for whom his writerly legacy is already assured. *Scrapbook* remains resoundingly Corderian, so his old readers will hear him roundly, unmistakably in the writing; appreciating the chance to revisit an old friend, they will pass over any imperfections. For those new to Corder, we hope that *Scrapbook* proves a neighborly introduction, enticing them to look and read further.

Let me finish my thanks and acknowledgments. Roberta Corder, as always, is a friend. So is Keith D. Miller, my colleague in preserving Corder's scholarly-creative legacy. Eric Knickerbocker, my co-editor, prepared the present text; James T. Jones, the manuscript's first text editor, made it readable; Eric Pervukhin, the book designer, made it beautiful. They all know the state of the original manuscript, part hand-written but mostly composed by manual typewriter. With Roberta Corder's permission, we reprint Jim's photographs and drawings (the latter mostly of family homesteads and barns). We wish we had the photos that Jim describes; lacking these, we have built a scrapbook of images reflecting the fragmentary nature of Corder's own narrative. Friends and family will recognize most, though we have resisted "naming" and dating them. Let them otherwise keep their mystery.

The introduction that follows situates Corder's memoir within the warring-twin themes of post-Jungian psychology and poststructuralist theory. It is scholarly, as one might expect from an English professor introducing a colleague's work. Yet readers are free to follow any of several paths. Those who find literary theory daunting, irritating, or simply irrelevant may skip the introduction entirely, cutting straight to the memoir. Alternatively, readers might detour through its brief, friendlier final section, "'Things Matter': Notes Toward the Saving of Postmodern Autobiography." Those of a more scholarly bent will want to work their way through the whole. Of course, Scrapbook stands on its own. One can confront memory, loss, self-deception, self-correction, and death without much theorizing or introduction. Suffice it, then, that Corder writes of growing up and aging while exploring problems of writing and identity within our own belated, skeptical, intellectually-weary times.

The Art of Corder's Scrapbook

I. Writing in the Afternoon of Life: Art and/as Therapy

> The art of life is the most distinguished and rarest of all the arts.
> —C. G. Jung, "The Stages of Life" (19)

In the introduction to *Selected Essays of Jim W. Corder,* Keith D. Miller calls attention to two features of Corder's style, his formulaic repetitions—Corder was, after all, a student of classical rhetoric—and his use of *epanothorsis,* the figure of self-correction.[1] True enough. Our essay begins, then, with an epigraph from C. G. Jung, whose description of mid-life reversals hints at the psychological urgencies underlying Corder's self-correcting rhetoric.

In his "Stages of Life," Jung offers the seminal discussion of mid-life crisis, that earth-shaking psychic event that jolts adults of their forties and fifties out of their previously comfortable, quasi-adolescent, quasi-unconscious state and into self-examination. Describing the pattern of human ego-development through mid-life, Jung offers an allegory of the sun's circuit. "In the morning," he writes, the sun "rises from the nocturnal sea of unconsciousness and looks upon the wide, bright world which lies before it in an expanse that steadily widens the higher it climbs in the firmament. In this extension of its field of action caused by its own rising, the sun will discover its significance; it will see the attainment of the greatest possible height ... as its goal" (14-15). Yet "at the stroke of noon the descent begins. And the descent means the reversal of all the ideals and values that were cherished in the morning. The sun falls into contradiction with itself. It is as though it should draw in its rays instead of emitting them. Light and warmth decline and are at last extinguished" (15).

The psychic and physical transformations occurring at mid-life (and continuing throughout one's aging) demand the reexamination, reappraisal, and, ultimately, reversal of ego-attitudes that had entrenched themselves during one's "first adulthood" (as Jungian analyst James Hollis terms it), though neither folk wisdom nor popular media offer sure guidance through this "middle passage" (Hollis 16)—that is, through life's transit toward an older and, one trusts, wiser "second adulthood." Rather, "thoroughly unprepared, we take the step into the afternoon of life; worse still, we take this step with the false assumption that our truths and ideals will serve us as hitherto" (Jung 16). But, Jung adds, "we cannot live the afternoon of life according to the programme of life's morning; for what was great in the morning will be little at evening, and what in the morning was true will at evening have become a lie" (16-17).

The programme of life's afternoon and evening requires our turning inward: "After having lavished its light upon the world, the sun withdraws its rays in order to illuminate itself" (Jung 17). Yet the goal of mid-life reaches beyond mere correction of youthful projections; as Jung suggests, "The afternoon of human life must also have a significance of its own" (17). Whereas the significance of life's morning "undoubtedly lies in the development of the individual" and in "the propagation of our kind" (17-18)—both of which serve "the obvious purpose of nature" (18)—life's afternoon turns away from mere "nature" in service of its spiritual opposite. "Money-making, social achievement, family and posterity are nothing but plain nature, not culture," Jung observes, and then follows with a question: "Could by any chance culture be the meaning and purpose of the second half of life?" (18). The delicacy of his questioning hints at the hazards such terms as "nature" and "culture" pose to postmodern consciousness. In earlier societies, Jung observes, "the old people are almost always the guardians of mysteries and the laws" (19), the transmitters of "cultural heritage" (19). Taking liberties with Jung's vocabulary, we might add that life's afternoon of "culture" (as opposed to the life of unconscious "nature") invests participants in a secular *cultus:* that is, in life lived ritually, spiritually, aesthetically, artistically.

It is the urge to re-experience life's mysteries through art—specifically, through the art of writing—that makes autobiography so important to modern culture generally and to Corder specifically. Memoir belongs to and serves the afternoon of life, providing not just an instrument of self-examination but a means of rendering artful—that is, meaningful—the previously unstudied experiences of one's "first adulthood." As Corder practices it, memoir becomes both art and therapy, renders art *as* therapy. Memoir becomes, arguably, the great spiritual (hence, artistic) task facing each older individual who strives for greater consciousness, though few take up the challenge as persistently as does Corder. For life-writing, particularly as Corder practices it, can never be easy.

Corder's own "middle passage" was rough. While in his fifties, he met with a succession of changes: separation from his first wife, divorce and remarriage (with estrangement from his older daughter), months-long hospitalization (with shock treatment) following a nervous breakdown, removal from the post of Vice Chancellor at Texas Christian University.[2] When he returned to the TCU English department to resume teaching, Corder had himself changed. And his writing followed suit. In a poignant confirmation of *enantiodromia*—Jung's idea that phenomena, initially one-sided, grow toward their opposites—Corder proceeded to rewrite virtually every aspect of his earlier rhetorical theory, as if to assert the equal validity of its negation.[3]

Though one-sided, the outward successes of one's "first adulthood" make inward change seem rash, unwarranted, dangerous, incomprehensible. As Jung writes,

> The nearer we approach to the middle of life, and the better we have succeeded in entrenching ourselves in our personal

attitudes and social positions, the more it appears as if we had discovered the right course and the right ideals and principles of behaviour. For this reason we suppose them to be eternally valid, and make a virtue of unchangeably clinging to them. (12)

In his late essay "Lessons Learned, Lessons Lost" (1995), Corder drives home this very point: "When you learn strong lessons early, however wrong, no evidence seems to count against them" (15). He goes on to say,

> How do you remember guilt, disgrace, honorable victory, honorable defeat, and success if the way you first learned them was maybe altogether wrong and certainly altogether mismatched to a world that any soul ever lived in? When persuasive people and daily evidence both testify otherwise, how do you continue to believe—and how wrong you would be if you did—that suffering is noble, that love is always accompanied by chivalric behavior, that the WASP family of 1934 is the appropriate goal of nostalgic dreaming, that true believers will at last be saved? (23)

Offering to correct the presumptions, prejudices, and ego-inflations of his "first adulthood," Corder—unlike Jung—implicates popular culture as their well-spring. Corderian self-correction thus proceeds as a critique of ideologies reigning throughout his Depression-era, West Texas youth—particularly the tired narratives of the American cowboy West, jingoistic patriotism, noble warfare, male machismo, and hell-fire religion, of all of which the youthful Corder proved too willing, too uncritical a consumer. The power of *Scrapbook* lies in its refusal to idealize and valorize the narrative subject—in thus demystifying the subject of autobiography.[4]

The task of life-writing for the postmodern intellectual is complicated further by contemporary theory's questioning of the very notions of individuality and identity. Through theory's withering skepticism, more than the hamlets and homesteads of Corder's youth disappear from the map: given poststructuralist declarations of the "death of the author," he writes as if expecting, at any moment, his own disappearance from the written page.[5] For Corder, then, autobiography becomes a distinctively post-Jungian enterprise.

II. Postmodern Autobiography and the Disappearing Author

> ... the ego ... is not even master in its own house ... .
>
> —Sigmund Freud, *Introductory Lectures on Psycho-Analysis* (353)

> And yet, and yet: I have written as much to hide as to reveal, have written so that I might show the writing to others and not be required to show myself. There's more to me than meets the eye, and less. Whatever is in here might be terrible to see, worse to reveal. A piece of writing can be revelatory, exploratory .... It can also be a substitute for the unspeakable, a closure, not a revelation.
>
> —Jim W. Corder, *Yonder* (54)

Scrapbook is a significant, arguably an important, experiment in postmodern autobiography. Here as in *Yonder* (1992), which we quote above, Jim plays the story-teller, arranging chapters in rough chronological order. Yet *Scrapbook* resists a reader's easy assumptions of narrative coherence, thematic unity, speed, and climax in life-writing. Approaching autobiography through residually Romantic aims and conventions, such a reader might expect human character to unfold and declare itself in a secure and knowable world, wherein one may project one's own life's possibilities. Such comforting projection is not the stuff of Jim's creative nonfiction, which is written "as much to hide as to reveal."

Throughout *Scrapbook*, such repetitions as "much is lost ... more is lost ... " and "I go looking. Where shall I look?" punctuate the narrative. Were these "mere" repetitions, *Scrapbook* might read like a broken record, each chapter stuck on the same losses, even if rehearsed in dif-

ferent times and settings. Yet Corder uses such phrasings to play variations upon his theme. For losses confront us everywhere during and after mid-life, from within and without. Beyond the cognitive ravages of
aging, one confronts a certain perversity of will that only selectively remembers some events while mis-remembering others; some memories,
as Freud reminds us, are lost to repression, actively (if unconsciously)
"forgotten," while others remain mere phantasms, wish-fulfilments pro-
jected upon a past that, put simply, did not happen—or, at least, did
not happen in quite that way.[6] And the past slips away externally, as
well. The West Texas hamlets of Corder's youth decay into ghost towns,
literally disappearing from maps; the dusty clapboard homesteads col-
lapse, rot away. Indeed, Corder goes looking for them; but where can
he look?

In "Losing Out" (1994), Corder acknowledges the poststructuralist
assault against selfhood:

> I am not a single, unitary, stable personality. I have composed
> myself and revised myself, always a little nostalgic for that oth-
> er self I could not compose, the one that sounds like Adrienne
> Rich, maybe, or Jacques Derrida, but looks like Gregory Peck.
> I am provisional and plural. (99)

Despite such acknowledgments, Corder could never embrace or con-
sent entirely to the current age's skepticism. He could admit the in-
stability and plurality of human identity; such admission does not,
however, free one from the responsibility—the duty, the urgency—of
self-making and life-writing. For regardless of poststructuralist efface-
ments, "We are still here," as Corder continues the passage immediately above, "responsible for ourselves though doubting ourselves. We
keep trying to tell our souls to the world. *We leave tracks*" (99; emphasis
added). More than a Derridean "trace" (that poststructuralist marker
of the writer's absence from his or her text), the "tracks" that Corder
describes mark the transformation (or, perhaps better, sublimation) of
external, material objects into personal symbols, anchoring memory
(and self-identity, however "provisional" and unstable) to the places

18

and particularities of lived experience. Cleansed of ideology and the misinterpretations borne of popular culture, such "tracks"—let us call them "memory-images"—become the stuff of Corderian autobiography, the subject of his searchings.

Detouring through the post-Jungian psychology of James Hillman, we can say that Corder's autobiography seeks recovery from the postmodern condition by seeking the numinous within lived experience, investing memory-images with the power of archetypes. Writing against the intellectual backdrop of postmodernism, Corder's solution to the problem of identity—however "provisional"—is implicitly mythic and archetypal.[7] "We keep trying to tell our souls to the world," he writes: though we have termed *Scrapbook* a postmodern autobiography, we could as well call it postmodern mythography, a "recovery of soul" (Hillman 15) by means of writing.

III. "Things Matter": Notes Toward the Saving of Postmodern Autobiography

> … and this feeling of being loved by the images … call this imaginal love.
> —James Hillman, *Archetypal Psychology* (14)

> But stories—histories, that is, and scrapbooks—can hold the blessed, ordinary particulars of creation. No truth waits otherwise.
> —Jim W. Corder, *Scrapbook*

"Things matter," Corder writes in "Lost Pieces," a middle chapter of *Scrapbook*. "Things," that is, the "blessed, ordinary particulars of creation"—the sum and substance of our stories—bear witness to our striving. By their means we seek ourselves, reach out to others, and hope for a legacy however threadbare and patchy, like fragments in a scrapbook or squares in a patchwork quilt stitched together in the here and now from the fabric of the then and there. Meanings dwell in the particulars, so we go searching for ourselves in the things that formed us, that continue to form us, collecting them, speaking them, turning them round in our minds: photographs that fade too soon, pages gathered and lovingly assembled in scrapbooks, selections of cloth carefully chosen and trimmed just so, the particulars quilted into a more or less unified whole though no less quilted for all of that, the only quilting these particulars—our particulars—will ever see.

"Things matter," Corder writes: "They make good weights to hold the world down, to keep memory and history from flying away in the wind." But how can we hold on to them, keeping them from flying away? How can we speak them? See them? "The light from the desk lamp," Corder notes, "catches in the heavy plastic frames of my glasses":

> I see what is before me, framed by that reflected light, as well as can be reasonably expected, but if I look up and out of the window, then I cannot see what is before me out yonder. I change glasses and see out there, but now I can no longer see what is before me here. When we make a new life, or stumble into a new life, we do so through the instrumentality of the old life. I find my far-seeing glasses by looking through my near-seeing glasses. I put on a new life and take up its instrumentalities. Then it's difficult to see the old life, or to find my other glasses. I do so eventually, looking, hunting, fumbling.

And sometimes in our fumbling, we are the ones seen and found out. As Rainer Maria Rilke writes in the first of his *Duino Elegies,*

> Yes—the springtime needed you. Often a star
> was waiting for you to notice it. A wave rolled toward you
> out of the distant past, or as you walked
> under an open window, a violin yielded itself to your hearing.
> All this was mission.
> But could you accomplish it? Weren't you always
> distracted by expectation, as if every event
> announced a beloved? (Where can you find a place

to keep her, with all the huge strange thoughts inside you
going and coming and often staying all night?)

For Corder, too, the "blessed, ordinary particulars" rise to greet us,
though our sight remains untrained: "We walk by burning bushes every day, but fail to notice. We walk in magnificence every day, but do
not notice. Sometimes, especially blessed, we lie down in magnificence,
but do not remark it."

Given their gloomy sentiments, the first two brief chapters may
challenge readers, requiring a leap of faith. Declarations of one's own
mediocrity may smack of depression and extreme ego-deflation, yet
Corder's resting place is one of affirmation, reconciliation, and hope.
Conversely, Corder's claim in ending chapters—that the world origi-
nates with him and will disappear with his own passing—is not hubris-
tic or ego-inflationary; it is, rather, an admission of the primacy of consciousness, of individual human imagination and experience. Symbols
of Selfhood—of emotional/psychic healing and wholeness, of reconciliation between Corder-the-child and Corder-the-man—lie scattered
throughout: buried tins, baseball gloves, West Texas sunsets, hill sides,
mesquite trees, ghost towns, dirt roads all take on archetypal meaning,
putting the narrator in touch with the Jungian "Self" or Soul.

Of particular note in Corder's lifelong Soul-questing is his struggle
to love—to value rightly the "anima" or archetypal feminine; he ex-
presses this struggle through dream imagery and fragments of memory,
including lost photographs. But of all the markers of Corder's Soul-
questing, the most poignant is his last: his description of his grandmother's quilt-making, whose intricate (yet home-made) patterns ex-
press the true American-folk mandala, symbolic of psychic wholeness.
For things do matter, especially through life's afternoon and evening,
when one's memory-images gather together, quilting.

Notes

1. Known alternatively as *metanoia* (in Latin, *correctio*), *epanorthosis* traces its pedigree back to Greek rhetorical tradition. The Elizabethan poet-rhetor, George Puttenham, offers the first extensive description in English, translating *metanoia* as "the penitent." Sometimes, Puttenham writes, "we speak and be sorry for it, … as if we had not well spoken, so that we seem to call in our word again, and to put in another fitter for the purpose: [and as] upon repentance commonly follows amendment, the Latins called it the figure of correction, in that the speaker seemeth to reform that which was said amiss" (223-24). Though quaint, Puttenham's description wonderfully anticipates Corderian practice, whose habit of self-correction transforms *epanorthosis* into a mode of verbal "repentance."

2. Corder hints at such events in *Scrapbook*. Toward the end of the chapter, "I Am Not Here," he recounts a visit with his second wife to Washington, D.C.:

> All the while, I wondered about my older daughter. Wherever I walked those days, she was somewhere within a couple of miles of where I was, but I didn't see her.… I paused halfway across the Taft Bridge to look at the autumn colors below and to look all around, wondering where she was, wondering, too, what would happen if she chanced to look out a window and see me walking along below. Would she want to catch up with me and visit? Would she turn away again? I guess I knew the answers.

Corder "knew the answers," though he leaves them unwritten: his oldest daughter had, after all, not forgiven him for divorcing her mother. In

the chapter "Vanished Places," Corder makes an offhand statement—
"I doubt that I'll go back to Galveston, where I once spent six months
in a daze"—left similarly unexplained. He refers to the time and place
of his hospitalization. Other such hints lie scattered throughout.

3. For discussion of the evolution of Corder's rhetorical theory, see
Baumlin, "Toward a Corderian Theory." In his *C. G. Jung Lexicon*,
Daryl Sharp describes *enantiodromia* as "typically experienced in
conjunction with symptoms associated with acute neurosis, and often foreshadow[ing] a rebirth of the personality" (51). As Jung writes
("Definitions," in *Collected Works* [1955] 6: ¶ 705), "This characteristic
phenomenon practically always occurs when an extreme, one-sided
tendency dominates conscious life; in time an equally powerful coun-
terposition is built up, which first inhibits conscious performance and
subsequently breaks through the conscious control" (qtd. in Sharp 51).

4. In a previous discussion (Baumlin, "Toward a Corderian Theory"),
one of us has described this aspect of Corder's creative nonfiction:

> Youthful, we strive to make a self, to make a strong person-
> ality, to marry, to make a career—to grow into the hero of
> our own story. The Corderian … *ethos,* in contrast, awakens
> to the guilty recognitions and regrets of older age, when one
> has lived long enough to amass a personal history of failures
> and (self-)deceptions. And what happens upon recognizing
> that the story we have told of ourselves "was maybe altogether
> wrong and certainly altogether mismatched to a world that
> any soul ever lived in?" In that crisis of mid-life and beyond,
> when our earlier, idealized self-image has proved to be little
> more than an occasionally pleasing fiction, are we not chal-
> lenged to reconstruct a self-image truer to our new sadder-
> wiser understanding of the world? What will this reconstruc-
> tion or "self-recovery" entail? For Corder, it necessitated not
> just the repudiation of his earlier, idealized self-image but the
> unmasking, debunking, and retelling of his entire life and

times: hence the personal narratives, *Lost in West Texas* (1988), *Chronicle of a Small Town* (1989), *Yonder* (1992), and *Hunting Lieutenant Chadbourne* (1993). (40)

5. "Writing," as Roland Barthes claims, "is that obliquity into which our subject flees, the black-and-white where all identity is lost, beginning with the very identity of the body that writes" (49); for, where "writing begins," "the voice loses its origin, the author enters into his own death" (49). Ever the English professor, Corder draws on the vocabularies of literary and rhetorical theory, particularly as these converge in notions of authorial *ethos*. In "The Scrapbook That Holds the Truth at the End of the World," the final chapter of his memoir, Corder confronts this aspect of recent theory, which combines "skepticism about the amount of control that a writer exercises over his or her work" with a "sharp sense of the fragility of personal identity," quoting the following from Alan Ryan (355):

> The idea that each of us is a single Self consorts naturally with the idea that we tell stories, advance theories, and interact with others from one particular viewpoint. Skepticism about such a picture of our identities consorts naturally with the thought that we are at the mercy of the stories we tell, as much as they are at our mercy. It also consorts naturally with an inclination to emphasize just how accidental it is that we hold the views we do, live where we do, and have the loyalties we do.

"If I stand against a classroom wall," Corder continues, "I tend to disappear. I am mostly sort of beige and grey, as are many institutional walls, and I'm likely to fade into the background of the moment. Perhaps I can argue myself into obsolescence and, with a little help, on into oblivion."

6. "Sigmund Freud was my father," writes Corder in the last chapter of *Scrapbook*. Quite so, for Freud sired us all intellectually, grounding our reigning theories of personality upon mechanisms of psychic defense

(unconscious wish-fulfilment, reaction-formation, sublimation, projection, repression). Much of *Scrapbook* reads, indeed, as self-analysis in the classic Freudian mode, replete with dream interpretation and free-association, dwelling upon sexual fantasy, hinting at half-disclosures and embarrassed confessions, returning obsessively to the scenes of "sins" that remain, nonetheless, "unspeakable." Given the power and pervasiveness of unconscious defenses, it would seem that memory—the underlying activity of life-writing—remains Herculean (rather, Sisyphean) in task. What makes Corderian memoir post-Freudian (again, postmodern) is its questioning of the narrative-analytic subject. As a "talking cure," psychoanalysis offers the hope of relief through storytelling; it cannot, however, guarantee ego-consciousness a stable, knowable, transcendent self-identity, independent of the stories it tells.

7. Playing freely with Hillman's discussion of dream-imagery, we can say that each place or object of Corderian life-writing, being transformed into a distinctive memory-image, "presents a claim—moral, erotic, intellectual, aesthetic—and demands a response" (Hillman 13-14). Such memory-images, as Hillman would say, "mean well for us, back us up and urge us on, understand us more deeply than we understand ourselves, expand our sensuousness and spirit, continually make up new things to give us" (14); indeed, this "message-bearing experience of the image—and the feeling of blessing that an image can bring—recalls the Neoplatonic sense of images as *daimones* and angels" (Hillman 14). We might compare Corder's claim that "stories—histories, that is, and scrapbooks—can hold the blessed, ordinary particulars of creation." Culminating *Scrapbook* with this claim, Corder takes this "blessing" seriously, the messengers of said blessing being the places and objects of memory: such are the *daimones,* the angels of Corderian memoir.

Works Cited

Barthes, Roland. "The Death of the Author." *The Rustle of Language.* Trans. Richard Howard. New York: Hill and Wang, 1986. 49-55.

Baumlin, James S. "Toward a Corderian Theory of Rhetoric." *Beyond Postprocess and Postmodernism: Essays on the Spaciousness of Rhetoric.* Ed. Theresa Enos and Keith D. Miller. Mahwah, NJ: Lawrence Erlbaum, 2003. 25-58

Corder, Jim W. *Chronicle of a Small Town.* College Station: Texas A&M UP, 1989.

———. *Hunting Lieutenant Chadbourne.* Athens: U of Georgia P, 1993.

———. "Lessons Learned, Lessons Lost." *Georgia Review* 46 (1992): 15-26.

———. "Losing Out." *Diversity: A Journal of Multicultural Issues* 1 (1993): 97-100.

———. *Lost in West Texas.* College Station, TX: Texas A&M UP, 1988.

———. *Yonder: Life on the Far Side of Change.* Athens: U of Georgia P, 1992.

Freud, Sigmund. *Introductory Lectures on Psycho-Analysis.* Trans. James Strachey. New York: Norton, 1966.

Hillman, James. *Archetypal Psychology: A Brief Account.* Dallas: Spring, 1983.

Jung, C. G. "The Stages of Life." *The Portable Jung.* Ed. Joseph Campbell. Trans. R. F. C. Hull. New York: Penguin, 1971. 3-22.

Miller, Keith D., and James S. Baumlin. "Introduction." *Selected Essays of Jim W. Corder: Pursuing the Personal in Scholarship, Teaching, and Writing.* Ed. James S. Baumlin and Keith D. Miller. Urbana, IL: NCTE, 2004 1-41.

Puttenham, George. *The Arte of English Poesie* (1589). Ed. Edward Arber. London: A. Constable, 1906. Rpt. Kent, OH: Kent State UP, 1970.

Rilke, Rainer Maria. *The Selected Poetry of Rainer Maria Rilke.* Trans. Stephen Mitchell. New York: Vintage, 1989.

Ryan, Alan. *John Dewey and the High Tide of American Liberalism.* New York: Norton, 1997.

Sharp, Daryl. *C. G. Jung Lexicon.* Toronto: Inner City, 1991.

What I Can Show and Tell

I'll begin with what I take to be a remarkable understatement. David Gerald Orr concludes his essay "The Icon in the Time Tunnel" (a discussion of secular and vernacular icons) with this remark:

> Who is making an effort to logically and consistently archive vernacular icons? Ironically, many icons of our own existence are ephemeral by nature and should be recorded. The alternative is a great cultural loss to generations of future historians and "iconographers."

I call this an understatement because the loss Orr speaks of is not just a loss to future historians and iconographers, but to all of us. The ephemeral he speaks of, objects of our everyday experience, are evidences of ourselves. From generation to generation they disappear. At any given moment they are mostly gone, for no one has saved them. With them are gone evidences of ourselves. The past is lopped off behind us. We try to remember, always absent complete archival storage. If there were complete storage of the artifacts of our lives, we'd not be able to use it, for it would overwhelm us. We have to select if we are to see, think, act, or talk. We will select, whether or not we intend to do so. ¶Much of our past is gone and with it vital sources of information about ourselves. Except, perhaps, for significant occasions, we cannot tell where we were at particular moments, or with whom we shared those moments. We cannot call back all the things we owned, touched, or coveted, or the clothes we wore. We can't remember all that we might have learned at church school or at funerals or at revival meetings. We do not know which texts really informed and directed our minds. (At moments, I think of the utter foolishness of the psychoanalyst's fifty-minute hour.

How shall therapist and clients ever learn anything without detailed and continuing research?) Much of our past is gone and with it vital sources of information about ourselves. Of what remains, we can only use a little at a time. ¶ The other's history is mostly hidden from us, and so is our own. The continuing autobiography that we are always saving in our heads, that always precedes and accompanies any utterance, is mostly gone. The sources, occasions, events, people, places, and things of the autobiography are mostly gone, and, oftener than not, we are gone, too, as we have learned, especially in the twentieth century, to eradicate most signs of personal authorship from what we say or write. Except for shards and scraps, our histories are gone, and our memories will not retrieve them. The only evidence I have of others, usually, is in the shape and style of what they say or show or tell. Of myself, I have some historical evidence as well, but it is incomplete. ¶ I can't tell myself to myself. I can't tell myself to you. You can't tell yourself to me. When I write or speak to myself or to you, I have already dropped off most of the history of what I say, therefore most of the meaning of what I say. ¶ Then what can we do? What can I do? ¶ Whether knowingly or not, we/I select what we can show and tell, what we have decided through continuing rhetorical transactions is real and can be shown or told. We live in and are continuing contests, some gentle and mild, some fierce and desperate, some entirely internal, self against self, some external, self against the other, contests in which we select what can be shown or told. Identity is a continuing rhetorical transaction as we negotiate our itineraries through the revealing though finally irrecoverable archives and through the structural and stylistic maneuvers by which we select what can be shown and told.

What I Can't Show and Tell

From time to time, I tell a dingy little story or try to recapture and to show a shoddy little episode in which I was a sorry and worthless participant. When I do so, I like to think that I am trying to be honest, trying to show a little why I see what I see and how I see what I see. But of course I can't. ¶I can't tell what I'm unwilling to say, what must not be said. ¶I can't show what would surely reveal me as a scoundrel in the private place where I live. ¶I can't tell my dearest and worst secrets. ¶I can't tell again the lies I've told. ¶I can't tell my profoundest sins, or the evil that I see in myself. ¶I can't tell my great embarrassments, woeful little episodes that make me cringe when I remember them. ¶I can't tell or show events and realizations that, recalled, are scarier to my soul than things that go bump in the night. ¶I can't tell or show what may be worse, how mediocre and insignificant I turned out to be.

Family

When you leave Aspermont, in Stonewall County, Texas, taking Highway 380 generally to the northwest, a little way out of town you pass a butte off to the south, and then you can see the Double Mountain. After seven or eight miles, you go through Swenson, which isn't there anymore, and 380 takes you now to the west. About five miles after you leave Swenson, a narrow road, FM 2211, turns south about two miles to Peacock, which mostly isn't there. From there, it was once possible to go generally west and across the Salt Fork of the Brazos for about two miles on a dirt road that doesn't have a number, then turn north for about two miles on another unnumbered dirt road to complete a little loop back to Highway 380. You can't make that loop anymore. The one-way wooden bridge over the Brazos has been out for some time, and I haven't seen any notable signs that it will be repaired. ¶The little stretch of dirt road that goes back north to Highway 380 would once have taken you to the Oriana community, legalized in the early part of this century by a post office, but long gone. I have not been able to find any trace of the community, but I have found the Oriana cemetery on a slope maybe half a mile west of the dirt road, a fenced-off piece of pasture. ¶I'd guess that there are fifty to sixty graves there. Almost all of them hold members of two families, the Kidds and the Bilberrys, though the latter shows up in three different ways on diverse

grave stones—Bilberry, Bilbery, and Bilbrey. My great-grandmother, the mother of my father's mother, is buried there. The gravestone says that she was Drew Silla Kidd. I never knew her. I don't know whether or not her name might have been Drusilla. Her daughter, Laura Kidd, my father's mother, my grandmother, is the only member of either family that I can remember, though I think I met some other Kidds and some Bilberrys when I was a boy. ¶Back out on Highway 380, if you go on west for two or three miles to the western edge of Stonewall County, you'll see a long slope stretching up to the north of the road. The one-room Center View School was near the road at the bottom of the slope. The Center View Church was at the top. At one time, I guess, there must have been several Kidd and Bilberry farms in that community, and for a while there must have been one Corder farm, my grandfather's place. I don't remember, or I never knew, any of those people or farms. In his poem, "After the Reunion," David Baker asks, "Who looks like who in the crisp old albums?" I don't remember any albums, only a few old photographs of people I didn't know. ¶I do remember one farm, however, that was to the north of Center View Church, just on the eroded edge of the gullies and canyons. I have been there recently. The house still stands, though it has probably been vacant for fifty or more years. The walls are weathered brown and gray. The chimney has caved in through the roof. The porch has fallen off. The fields around the house have long since gone to sparse grass and thick mesquite. This was the Durham place, where my other grandfather sharecropped. He and my grandmother lived there with my mother, her four sisters, and their brother. My mother and my father first met at Center View School. They were married in 1924. ¶I have one studio portrait of their family made when we were all young. One member is missing. My little sister would not be born for another twelve years or so after the picture was made. The four of us are posed nicely in the photographer's studio, which, "equipped with a variety of painted backgrounds against which clients could pose," as Julia Hirsch puts it, " … has offered the family photographic refuge from its own history." I can't tell a lot about the background here; I expect that was intentional. To the picture's upper left there appear two vaguely church-like arched

windows, with trees suggested through them. The background otherwise is mostly dark. ¶The picture was made perhaps as early as 1932. The little male child that must be me appears to be about three years old. ¶My mother stands in the center of the picture. If I am right about the date of the picture, she is twenty-four or twenty-five, and she looks good, though she is heavier than in the pictures I mentioned earlier. Her hair is somewhat obscured against the dark background, but I do believe that she has just had what they used to call a permanent. Her dress is moderately dark (perhaps a blue or green), and I judge that it is silk. It has a lace inset collar and long lace sleeves extend past the elbow length. She is looking directly into the camera. My father sits to her left (the picture's right) on a lace-covered stool. He is twenty-six or twenty-seven. He is a pretty man. His hands are clasped in his lap. He wears a dark suit with a vest. His shoes are well shined. My brother, who must be about eight, stands to the right and a little in front of my mother, on the picture's left. He looks pretty much as he ought to look. He wears a white shirt with a tie and knee pants with ankle socks. I can't distinguish anything about his shoes. I'm standing in the middle, in front of my mother, between my father and my brother. My left arm rests on my father's knee. I don't reach as high as my mother's waist, and she wasn't tall. I'm wearing a shirt and a sleeveless sweater, but I can't make out anything else, for I'm mostly behind my father's knee. My hair is quite blonde, almost white. Now my hair is mostly bald-colored, with fringes of white and gray and what my mother once called turd-muckledy-dun. ¶I know those other three. They look as they are supposed to look, the way I remember them from those times and later, until I discovered that they were old. I'm not so sure about the image of myself. That child might have become somebody else.

garbled reading of ourselves in the minds of others,
at first fuzzy, then inaccurate, then forgotten.
We can't hold the world still in our hearts
or pockets. "Settling my account with the
past," Randy Blasing writes, "only amounts to
adding up my losses." A photograph will hold
only a moment. "The rest," William Trowbridge
says,

> as we're sometimes told, belong to history,
> off camera, clearing its ~~throat~~ rheumy throat.

~~Sometimes our own language stays us from~~
~~Our own language stays us from keeping the~~
~~particulars of our world.~~
Sometimes, if not always, our own language stays
us from keeping the particulars of our world. In
a review of Leo Bersani's The ~~Culture of~~ Culture
of Redemption, John Scurrock remarks that the
absolutely singular is betrayed when a novelist,
for example, uses it ~~to exemp~~ only to exemplify a
truth or design, annihilating reality in the interest
of philosophy. Then he asks, "But how is any
writer to represent to us the absolutely singular
when representation itself requires symbols, ~~su~~ such
as those of language, which are absolutely not
singular?" "Even though we know," John Berger
says, "that no two blades of ~~gr~~ grass are alike,
the word 'grass' suggests an identity." Berger
continues:

What is Lost (I)

We can't keep the world, and we can't stay in the world. Jodi Daynard remarks "that paper crumples, ink fades; that the bold handwriting of youth inevitably yields to the childish scrawl of old age. Soon, very soon, manuscripts seem to tell us, we will be nothing more than the papers—or printouts—we leave behind." And they, I'll add, will be generally lost and forgotten. ¶We can't stay in the world. If anything remains, it will be only dim images and garbled readings of ourselves in the minds of others, at first fuzzy, then inaccurate, then forgotten. We can't hold the world still in our hearts or pockets. "Settling my account with the past," Randy Blasing writes, "only amounts to adding up my losses." A photograph will hold only a moment. "The rest," William Trowbridge says,

> As we're sometimes told, belongs to history,
> Off camera, clearing its rheumy throat.

Sometimes, if not always, our own language stays us from keeping the particulars of our world. My mind wants to stay in and with particulars, but I lose blades of grass from my mind, can't keep how they look, as I lose them in words, little class notes from life. Words, someone else reminds me, aren't reality, and I reply, quietly, that they are, that they are our only hold, else we lose the evidences of ourselves. We can't remember without words. I can't keep any trace of reality for myself without words, or tell any trace to another. I guess that there will never be complete archival storage of all the dear, sweet, odd, threatening people and places and things of creation, though sometimes I wish that there were and that I could rummage through it all at will. ¶My good friend, now gone, and I used to argue occasionally about essays. "There

never was an essay written and published," he'd say, "that couldn't have been shorter." Then I'd say, "There never was an essay written and published that shouldn't have been longer." He was right. He was a good editor, he liked crisp, economical prose, and he liked to get to the point. ¶I don't think creation comes to a point. A point is what's left after you whittle all else way. A point is a dot on a map that locates a town you've reached after you've missed the countryside. I don't want to reduce to a point. I have wanted to enlarge toward life. I can't. Too much is lost.

Sisters

I.

The picture came in a letter from Aunt Cora, postmarked February 10, 1988. I have not pondered it constantly since, or regularly, or even frequently, but I have come back to it again and again. The picture shows a ghostly gathering. Of the six people imaged there, three are dead; the other three are waiting to die, two in what some would call a nursing home, what others would call a retirement center, the last at home, almost blind, generally incapacitated. Even if all were alive, active, and talkative, they would still make a ghostly gathering: I do not know them, but I have heard them all my life and have known them. The picture shows my mother, her four sisters, and her brother when they were still children. ¶The picture measures five inches by seven inches, with a quarter-inch border on all sides. The larger measure of the height accommodates a modest vertical arrangement of the six children on what appear to be the steps of a porch. That is confirmed by Aunt Cora, if her memory can be trusted any more than mine. In her letter, she says that "I am sending you a picture of all of us that I had blown up from a very small Kodak picture that was made on our back porch before we moved to West Texas." She more or less confirms my guess about their ages. They moved to West Texas, I believe, in 1919, when boll weevils destroyed Grandpa's young cotton crop. My mother was born in 1907. I guess she couldn't have been more than eleven, going toward twelve in the fall. That works out all right. Cecil, the baby, whom she is holding beside her on the step, looks to be about one, and the two of them were born about ten years apart. She is eleven, then, in the picture. ¶What is there is what was framed by the camera, and the frame doesn't hold the content of the instant. My mother, my aunts, and my uncle are in the light there on the steps, yes, five little girls and a baby boy, and in their faces, except for his, I can see who they would be when I came to know them, but much is unrevealed. I can't see who held the camera; I can't see what they are looking at, off to their right. I am unable to learn the occasion for the snapshot. I can't get into "before the picture," or "after the picture." I can't get outside the picture. I can't get into the picture, either: they're there in the light on the steps of the porch, but I don't know these children. ¶The adults they became I knew too little: Uncle Cecil, Aunt Nell, Aunt Cora, Aunt Bill, Aunt Edith, my mother. Images flit about in my head, but their histories are gone from me, were never present. I hope that the persisting images have some close relation to whatever may have happened. The photograph doesn't show Uncle Cecil's ease and grace when he jumped the yard fence that time he came to see us; such thrilling ease and grace, I thought then, in the second grade, that I'd never be able to achieve. The photograph doesn't show the chicken snake Aunt Cora and I found that time in the hen's nest, lumps down its body where the whole swallowed eggs were. Aunt Cora was pretty pissed. When it came to doing pretty pissed, Aunt Cora was world class. The photograph shows that two of the children had light hair, but it doesn't show that when they grew up to be Aunt Edith and Aunt Bill, their hair was the color of enchantment, a pale and lovely reddish gold. The photograph doesn't show Aunt Edith's elegance, or her coconut cream pie, doesn't show that Aunt Bill was lovely, that her secret, serene smile marked her, in my mind, apart from the others. ¶Images flit and flicker. ¶When I was young and all of the family gathered on a holiday—Christmas, say—at my grandparents' farm, the outhouse there was the centerpiece for a regular entertainment. It was the custom of the gathered cousins—I don't know how many there were, and I believe that on two different occasions strangers joined the gathering undetected—to spend a portion of one morning chunking rocks at the outhouse. When it was empty, this was practice; when it was occupied, this was fun. It was a game that required both skill in the throwing arm and keen judgment, for some of the adults, when they went to the outhouse, wouldn't do as targets. Aunt Edith, for example, and Aunt Bill were both entirely too gentle and refined, too ladylike, for us to intrude upon their world. Any uncle would do. But Aunt Nell was out of bounds for particular and practical reasons: she was too young and frisky; she would chunk rocks back at us when she came out, she had a good arm and a sure aim, and she could whip most of us at wrestling. Aunt Cora, though, was just right. If we threw rocks at the outhouse while she was in it, she could be counted on to roar and bellow at us from inside and then to emerge with the proper bluster and simulated rage. ¶Other images of Aunt Nell flicker uncorrected in my mind. Later, she was a nurse. Once, when an unlettered farmwoman with too many children asked her about contraception, Aunt Nell told her, "Honey, you're going to have to take orange juice, and you're going to have to be faithful and regular about taking it." ¶"Well," the woman asked, "when do I take it, before or after?" ¶"Instead of," Aunt Nell said. About a year later, the woman was back at the Spur hospital to have another baby, and she asked again about contraception. ¶"Orange juice just didn't work, huh?" Aunt Nell said. ¶"Couldn't always afford to keep orange juice," the woman said. ¶"Well, do you have a big old bucket out at your place?" ¶"Yes, we do," the woman said. ¶"Honey, you're going to have to take that bucket to bed with you every night." ¶"But what'll I do with it?" ¶"The minute you get in bed," Aunt Nell said, "you put both your feet in it and sleep that way." ¶Serious advice followed both times, Aunt Cora said. She's the one who told me the story. ¶One time Aunt Nell came to see us in Fort Worth. I don't remember the year—it was early in World War II, and I was maybe thirteen. My family had moved there from West Texas, and we didn't go back because gas was rationed and our tires were thin and our car was old. Since it was summer and school was out, my parents said I could drive back to West Texas with Aunt Nell and stay with my grandparents at the farm. The moon was full and big beyond imagining at our back. The moonlight was bright and clean and lovely, and the world was clear, and there were no cars but ours on the road. In the long stretch between Mineral Wells and Breckenridge, Aunt Nell decided that the moonlight was so bright she believed she could just about drive without the headlights on, and so she did. I thought it was exciting and brave and beautiful, and rode for miles in the clear world, enthralled. ¶That was a long time ago. Aunt Nell died in December 1985. She was a long time dying. We had planned that I would drive my parents to Levelland, where Aunt Nell lived, for the funeral. But when the time came, an ice storm had moved across the state, the roads were sheeted and slick, and we were not able to get to where she was. I never did get to where she was, I guess; never learned her story; wasn't sure what she was like when I was watching; never knew what she was like when I wasn't looking, but I remember riding with her in the bright moonlight. ¶The photograph doesn't show my mother. It shows a little girl, caught with her eyes closed, there on the unpainted porch steps of an unpainted house, a little girl who had, I'd guess, no dream of my father, my brother, my sister, or me. I wonder what she did dream. I do not learn from the picture what gave her strength to end her life when she was tired of it, some three months after my father died. ¶I don't know these children, or the adults they became. I always see them with my eyes, through my memory, out of my ways of thinking and seeing. All of them get away from me. If we all got together—Lynette, Karen, and Elise, the children of Cecil; Duane and Beryl, the children of Edith; Harvey and Card, the children of Bill; Nell and Danette, the children of Nell; Eddie and Marilyn, the children of Cora; Nolan, Sandra, and me, the children of Ruth—we'd learn new stories from each other about each of them, the fictions we agree upon as family history. But we wouldn't catch them; they slip away.

2.

I think of what is lost that I know is lost, minutes, hours, days, weeks, that I have forgotten. What I have forgotten, even if it was dailyness, may have been momentous. How can I understand the lesson of my life if I don't know where they came from, don't know how and when and why I learned them? I think of what is lost that I don't know is lost. What people, places, events are so lost to me that I don't even know I've forgotten? Or never knew?

3.

The first picture came from Aunt Cora. Two other pictures that show them all together came from my mother. The three pictures came to me late. Aunt Cora sent the first picture not long before she died, and

46

late in my life. I had never seen it before. The other two came from my mother's collection after she died, and late in my life. I had seen them before, but I had never looked at them. When I do look at them, they don't seem to be what I might have expected, though I'm not sure what I expected. ¶As Julia Hirsch says in *Family Photographs,* such pictures "delude, obscure, or reveal, but never leave us entirely neutral. They are always relics which remind us of what we had forgotten, make us want to forget what we remember, and bring into relief what we already knew." Moreover, Hirsch says, family photography "sustains the notion of the family as a corporate entity,"

> and the concept of the family as a corporation which no individual will or ego can pull asunder is one of enormous social utility and psychological appeal. It assures us that the family, as an institution, can overwhelm and control our most confused impulses by promoting the triumph of community over self, of history over moment, of the "haven in a heartless world."

But here I cannot see any clear sign of unity and coherence. Nor can I see any sure indication of proper relationships among them. The family seems to have no notion, as Hirsch puts it, "of how a family ought to look: the father, authoritative, the mother, tender, the child, protected." And I cannot locate them in these pictures, as Hirsch suggests we usually can: "The places we photograph are our roots. Family photographs are taken in backyards, front of the house, in the driveway … and wear out as we move through our lives as children, siblings, spouses and parents." ¶If something is wrong in these two pictures, if they do not seem to know how a family is supposed to look, if they seem unaware of the conventions of family photography, I have, of course, no way of knowing whether it is owing to the artlessness of the photographer, to unexpected movement or "disorderly conduct," to some momentary problems, or to something strange and dark in the nature of the family. ¶The first of the two pictures from my mother's collection is a snapshot, measuring four and a half by two and a half inches, including border. The picture shows my mother, her sisters, her brother, and their par-

and their parents, my Grandma and Grandpa Durham. It is not as troublesome to me as the ~~co~~ second picture, but it is troublesome.

I cannot tell where they are. What's visible of the yard is dirt. The family is standing immediately in front of a picket fence that tilts a little. Just beyond the fence and behind the family is a large mesquite. Off to the right and farther away is a smaller mesquite. The upper rail of the fence obscures the prairie horizon. To judge from their ages, I guess they must be in West Texas, perhaps near Center View, which no longer exists as a community. My mother, I guess, is maybe fifteen, my uncle Cecil may be five, the other four between them. Perhaps it's about 1922. Grandma and Grandpa, inconceivably to me, might still be in their early forties. Grandma wears a dark dress with a lace collar. Grandpa wears a suit, a white shirt, and a tie. My mother wears a dark skirt and what appears to be a dressy, partly sheer, white blouse. The ~~f~~ other four sisters, Edith, Bill, Cora, and Nell, wear variations of shirt-waist dresses. Cecil wears dark shorts and a white, little-boy-dress-up white shirt with a wide Fauntleroy collar.

It's how they have arranged themselves, or been arranged, that puzzles me a little, or

ents, my Grandma and Grandpa Durham. It is not as troublesome to me as the second picture, but it is troublesome. ¶I cannot tell where they are. What's visible of the yard is dirt. The family is standing immediately in front of a picket fence that tilts a little. Just beyond the fence and behind the family is a large mesquite. Off to the right and farther away is a smaller mesquite. The upper rail of the fence obscures the prairie horizon. To judge from their ages, I guess they must be in West Texas, perhaps near Center View, which no longer exists as a community. My mother, I guess, is maybe fifteen, my uncle Cecil maybe five, the other four between them. Perhaps it's about 1922. Grandma and Grandpa, inconceivably to me, might still be in their early forties. Grandma wears a dark dress with a lace collar. Grandpa wears a suit, a white shirt, and a tie. My mother wears a dark skirt and what appears to be a dressy, partly sheer, white blouse. The other four sisters, Edith, Bill, Cora, and Nell, wear variations of shirtwaist dresses. Cecil wears dark shorts and a little-boy-dress-up white shirt with a wide Fauntleroy collar. ¶It's how they have arranged themselves, or been arranged, that puzzles me a little or disturbs me. They are in two rows of four. The row in back, pretty close to the picket fence, includes from left to right, Aunt Edith, my mother, Grandpa, and Grandma. In front of them stand Uncle Cecil, Aunt Nell, Aunt Bill, and Aunt Cora. But it might be better to say that they stand in four groups of two: Cecil in front of Edith, Nell in front of my mother, Bill in front of Grandpa, Cora in front of Grandma. The picket fence and clear space are visible between each pair. They are clearly not touching side to side and do not appear to be touching front to back. All save Edith and Bill stand square to the camera. Edith and Bill have turned to their left. Bill is still looking at the camera, but Edith has turned almost 45 degrees from the camera and appears to be ignoring the occasion. I wonder whether or not being a strawberry blonde makes you stand aslant from the others. I wonder why space surrounds each of them. I wonder why they are not touching each other. ¶The other picture is more troublesome and disturbing. ¶The picture measures about five inches by three inches, including a border. I can't determine either the time or the place. At the right of the picture, or to their left, a single post of a barbed wire fence is visible. Bare limbs of a small tree rise behind the family, and above to their left. Beyond, a flat to rolling prairie goes to the horizon just above their elbows. They might even be at the farm I remember. They might be elsewhere. I'd guess the picture was made perhaps as early as 1932, when the six children would have ranged in age from Cecil at about fifteen to my mother at about twenty-five, perhaps as late as 1935. All of them begin to look as I remember they looked when I began to be aware of them. ¶They form a ragged row. Grandpa is at the left side of the picture. Grandma is next. Then come my mother, Edith, Bill, Cora, Nell, and Cecil. Judging from the way their clothes have blown, I'd say that they face into the wind. ¶But if they form a ragged row, they do not form a group. They separate. ¶Grandpa is at the left. He is turned right shoulder to the front, about forty-five degrees to the camera, though he appears to be looking directly at it. He is isolated from the rest. The tail of his coat has blown back almost enough to touch Grandma's coat sleeve. ¶I'll come back to Grandma in a moment. ¶The six children do form a group, arranged in a modest arc composed of my mother, Edith, Cora, Nell, and Cecil, with Aunt Bill in the center and slightly in front. All are nestled close and look-ing at the camera. My mother at the left end and Uncle Cecil at the right have turned slightly to close the arc, and it excludes Grandpa and Grandma. ¶Grandma is alone, separated from both Grandpa and her children. She has turned to her right, so that she is almost at ninety de-grees to the camera, and her back is to her children. She faces Grandpa, but she isn't looking at him. Her eyes are closed. She looks hurt or grim. I never saw her sweet, powdery face grim, but she might have been fre-quently grim when I wasn't looking. Perhaps she has only turned away from the wind in her eyes. Something is wrong. ¶A snapshot, Hirsch suggests, will tell us "only the barest of narratives." I have no photo-graphs of my father's family all together. Or of my own.

4.

I wonder what I knew of them that is lost now to my memory. I won-der what is lost of them that I never knew.

5.

Perhaps not showing immediately, but soon enough evident, a hiatus has occurred here, and not only can I not find what is lost to my memory or what is lost because I never knew it, but now I cannot find the myself that was. ¶As I am able to recapture the sequence of events, when I had put down the few words that are shown above as section 4, some other little projects interrupted what I had supposed I was thinking about. Now, some fifteen months have passed. While I am glad to take note that I have not died in the meantime, I am sometimes mystified when I return to the files and notes with which I first began. ¶I don't imagine myself to be an explorer of lost worlds, though each of us surely is, or an archeologist, or the first reader of the Rosetta Stone, but the files and notes do have about them the quaintness, if not of hieroglyphics, at least of an antique language that I can't entirely decipher. Neither do I imagine myself to be a marvel of depths that must be plumbed and breadths that must be ranged. Still, the files and notes do puzzle me a little. ¶Perhaps I expected to find there a structure of meaning in which I could situate myself again. Perhaps I supposed that if I could locate myself in some system of thought, then I would find what I reckoned I was thinking and where I believed I was going. Perhaps I even hoped that this system of thought, if I could get back into it, would enable me to locate and identify myself irrefutably. ¶I don't much think so now. If I manage to locate something that looks like a self, it will not be the same self that made the notes and files, though my character is not large enough to house multitudinous changes. And if there is a system of thought, someone else will find it, and I'll be gone.

6.

I have other snapshots, and I often think of the snapshots that I don't have, of those that were never taken. Of studio photographs, however, I have fewer than a handful, and do not regularly see many more. ¶One that I do see hangs in my sister's house. It shows my sister and me, and I expect it must have been taken in 1948, when she was three and I was eighteen. We were temporally scattered: our brother was

already twenty-three and long gone into his own family. That left my little sister and me. When my mother became visibly pregnant some fifteen years after bearing me, she stopped going to the Baptist church until after my sister was born. I guess that she didn't want folks to know that she and my father had been messing around. ¶ The studio photograph measures eight inches by ten inches. She is on the left, I on the right, as I look at the picture. I think perhaps I was sitting down and she was standing close against my right shoulder. The photograph appears to be in color, but I believe it was in black and white, enhanced by whatever technology then allowed photographs to be tinted. I have been considerably beautified by the process, but she was beautiful at the outset. We were close. We were pretty silly about each other. ¶ But shortly after the photograph was made, she and I parted. My father was transferred, and he and my mother and my little sister moved. I stayed behind to go to school. Now, when I look at the picture, call back that time, Rodney Jones's poem, "For My Sister," reminds me that

As our bodies grew into strangers,
There were no words.

About ten years later we all came to the same city to live, the three of them and myself, now with my own family. My little sister still lives across town. We love each other and enjoy each other, but each of us, I think, has a hole in life. Even now, we sometimes fall into its darkness when we remember what we missed of each other. "Soon," Yehuda Amichai says,

of the two of us, neither will be left
to forget the other.

7.
I had a small black-and-white snapshot of a beautiful young woman, but I no longer know where it is. Perhaps I've lost it. Yes, I've lost it. The picture shows her standing in the ruins of a bombed out building in Mannheim, Germany. At the time, in the spring of 1952, she was

twenty-three. She is beautiful. She opened to me, and her love was fair. She was my sister, my bride. I denied her and turned away, and the picture is gone.

8.

I have few photographs of my daughters when they were young, and few since. I used to scoff at parents who, I thought, spent a good part of their time making home movies or videos or photographs of their children. I would scoff at them and say, maybe, "Looks to me like they spend more time making pictures of their children than they do looking at them." Perhaps I really felt that way. Perhaps not. Perhaps that was only a way of hiding the anxiety and lonesomeness I felt almost from the start when I looked at the children: one day they would go away. The act of making a photograph eliminates another photograph that may have been made. Which moment shall I save? Cathy in the fourth grade in red plaid and red tights, the star of her school play? Mindy with her violin, revealed as the curtain rose to start the show that she starred in when she was a college sophomore, sitting on the make-believe roof of a make-believe house, playing the theme from *Fiddler on the Roof?* Which moments should I have saved? Every single moment that was or will be counted. I wish I could have every moment. I can't.

9.

On my desk, there is a four by six inch color snapshot of my wife. She is walking on the beach behind the Eden Roc Hotel in Miami Beach. She is wearing a tee shirt and, though it's not visible, a bathing suit. I think her legs are lovely. The water line runs from the lower left of the picture to the upper right. Her head is down. Someone who does not know her might think that she is dejected. She is not on this day. She is looking for treasures along the beach. She finds treasures everywhere. She has made an art gallery of our house, a delight of my life. For brief moments on some days, as when looking at this picture, I am a little sad, wishing I could have known her when she was a girl and a young woman, could have seen and known all she saw, all she did, all she thought. After all this time, I am just beginning to find and to know her. I'll never have time enough for all I want of that.

10.
In one of her poems, Linda Pastan reminds me that I have only a single hoe to dig up all of Eden or whatever patch I find. Much is still covered over that I know is lost. Much is still covered over that I never knew was lost. Overblown with red dirt and tumbleweeds, much is lost because I went off and left it.

What Is Lost (II)

And so I slowly began to learn that when I itemized what is lost, I didn't go far enough. Much of our culture's past is gone. Most family histories are gone. Most of the sources of vital information about ourselves is gone. I don't know where I was on a Friday in 1944, on a Tuesday in 1967, or with whom. What things surrounded me? What were my clothes really like? Toys? Sunday school lesson pamphlets? What school books did I read and believe? ¶ But I can add one more item to my list. ¶ Much is lost that I know is lost. More is lost that I don't know is lost because I never knew it. Much is lost that I went off and left. Much is lost that, in willful ignorance, I chose not to see.

Brothers

Now, turning through newspapers, I pause
to see if anyone who passed away
was younger than I am…. Nothing matters
enough to stay bent down about….
Dying matters a little. So does pain.
So does being old. Men do not.
Men live by negatives, like don't give up,
don't be a coward, don't call me a liar,
don't ever tell me don't…. What's man but a
match, a little stick to start a fire with?
—Miller Williams

I had thought I'd be Digby, the middle one, faithful and ready. We had no John, no youngest brother, in our family. My brother was Michael, the oldest, the best, Beau Geste. I thought family should stay together, close, intent on love and fidelity, as they were. I forgot to keep the covenant. I'm the one. Later, with a somewhat larger cast of characters, I forgot again, or failed. I'm the one. But the three of them, Michael, Digby, and John, told the way being and brothering and gallantry were supposed to be, while I waited to be good Digby, old Dig. ¶You remember the story of Percival Christopher Wren's *Beau Geste*. I had it first from my father's recommendation and the book, but Gary Cooper died for its sake; and later, in various remakes, some younger fellows did, too. You remember the story: how, to save the family, Lady Barbara sold the rare Blue Water without telling anyone and kept a false gemstone in its place; how, to save Lady Barbara's reputation, Michael, rare Beau, stole the false gem and, thought a criminal, fled to France to join the Foreign Legion; how good Digby, steady Dig, to save rare Beau's reputation, said he stole the gem, fled to France to claim the guilt; how young John, steady John, to save the names of rare Beau and steady Dig, said he stole the gem, fled to France, and found them;

how they went to Africa with the legion; how they practiced war; how two died; how one came back to tell the story. ¶They told what brothering was, I thought: selfless, forthright, always close. They defined gallantry. Beau watched over young John and died. Young John laid him out there at Fort Zinderneuf. Digby put a dog at his feet and set the flames for a Viking's funeral and then went forthright to die for young John. ¶I thought it was the way. My brother was Michael, the best, Beau Geste. I had no flair, no wit, but I was willing and would be Digby. We had no John to tell the story. It was the way I thought being and brothering should be, and were, while I waited to be good Digby, old Dig. ¶Later, I was startled to find that most of humankind had not received the vision. The brothers had defined brothering, I thought, and gallantry, and I was surprised into regret when I learned that the book was as slight as myself, and very nearly as new, published in 1926, some three years before my parents published me. ¶Still, it was the way I thought being and brothering and gallantry were, while I waited to be old Dig. But then we had no John to tell the story, my brother didn't know that he was Beau, and after a while I forgot to be Digby. ¶When I was a boy, I called my brother *Son*. All of us did, our parents, assorted cousins, aunts, and uncles. When my wife later learned about that, she didn't care much for the practice. "What did they think *you* were?" she asked. As the years passed, all the others learned to call him by his proper name. I still call him Son because to me that is his proper name, though we're sixty years from being the boys we were when I first learned to call him that. He is five years older than I am, and then I thought he was always grown, knowledgeable, strong, and heroic, and he always was except later when he wasn't. I don't think about my brother as often as I think I should. Perhaps he doesn't often think of me. When we do think of each other, perhaps each of us catches the wrong brother. He was always grown, knowledgeable, strong, and heroic, but the little photograph I have of his high school football team shows that he was a boy. ¶When he was a boy, I called my son *David*. I still do, and he's still a sweet boy, though because of him I am long since a grandfather. Once in a while, especially on the telephone for some reason, I call him *Buddy*. In my office, I have an eight by ten inch glossy photograph of him at bat in a ball game. He is most of the way through his swing, he has already connected, and the ball has already gone. His eyes are still focused on where the ball and his bat come together. The muscles in his arms distinguish themselves. He probably doesn't think of himself as a sweet boy. Our images of each other don't always coincide with who each of us imagines he is. Sometimes, I believe, he thinks I am big and strong and occasionally wise. Mostly, though, I guess he knows that "all boys are orphaned," as Michael Blumenthal puts it,

When they turn to speak their father's name
and a mere man answers.

A Dream of Children

A woman is speaking, as if in reverie. Her voice is sweet. She is lovely and graceful. She wears a dress of many soft colors, mostly, I think, blues and greens. She is in the sun room of a large manor house, and I know we are in England. The room is light; it appears to have windows on three sides. Growing plants are potted here and there around her, and she is arranging bright flowers in a vase. She is, perhaps, in her mid-forties. ¶No, she is not speaking. I hear her thinking. Her voice is still sweet. She is Christopher Robin's mother, and Pooh might be close by. Two young girls, daughters, I'm certain, perhaps nine and twelve, play around her. The room is festive, gay as if for a birthday party. There are balloons and bubbles, and bright colors swirl in the air. We are in England, though I may not be visible. I know that it is, perhaps, 1916, and I know, too, that her son, older brother to the two young girls, has long since gone off to war. ¶She speaks, her voice still sweet, and I hear her thinking, "Won't it be lovely, girls, when Tom comes home?" ¶Some interruption, some movement, occurs, some moments have passed. Then I learn that the girls, though I thought that they were busy playing, have also heard her, whether she speaks or thinks. The younger girl looks up from what she is doing, turns to the woman, and says or thinks, "Tom won't be coming home, Mother. Remember?" ¶Another break occurs, some sharper change. The scene may be the same. I see the windows, I believe, but the balloons and bubbles are gone. The air is still colors, more vivid now, and whirling faster. If the scene is the same, it is disturbed now, no longer festive and gay. The sweet woman has gone. The younger girl has gone. The older daughter is now the speaker or thinker. She is troubled and disturbed. No, the older daughter has gone, too. Cathy, my older daughter, is now the speaker or thinker, and she is more than troubled and disturbed. She is forlorn, bereft, almost frantic, as if she has been running here and there. Now I know that she does not speak, and I know that she is forlorn and bereft because she has not been able to catch or to gather or to reap or to hold or to keep the mustard.

Such was my dream one night in Mexico City. I am not, of course, certain that I have caught the details well. I can account only in small ways for pieces of this dream and for my role in it. Out of the dream, I can scarcely account for myself at all. ¶But dreams are archives, too, though mostly they can't be kept. ¶The first segment of the dream is set in England, which may, of course, stand for some setting that I can't discern. However, it is not surprising that I should find myself there, watching, hearing. I have studied and taught at, in, and around English literature for almost forty years. I did not include it in my recollection of the dream, but I remember thinking (I believe as I was waking) that all of this was an episode that had been omitted from one of the Winnie-the-Pooh books. I called Catherine *Pooh* when she was a baby, and my son and both daughters read the books. There may be a simpler explanation for the setting. The day before the dream, while my wife was at a lunch for the conference she was attending, I ate at a restaurant next to our hotel. The restaurant billed itself as, and almost was, an English pub. The Yorkshire pudding was good. The two girls may be surrogates for my daughters, also three years apart in age. Why was war introduced into the dream? I cannot be certain. War may be here as a way of getting to loss, but it is not surprising that a male of my age could have war stored away somewhere in the mind. Most of us learned warrior expectations early, and we learned lessons that went deep and stayed, even when we later learned better, about what is required of one if he is to be a man. ¶What I take to be the loss of the son in war, occurring in the daughter's painful reminder to her mother, is not surprising, either in the dream or in England in 1916. Over the years, I have, I expect, spent an unwise amount of time reading about wars and losses, great and small losses. I can't account for this beyond reckoning that early I thought it was honorable to go to war, then I wondered how young men could bear to go to war, then I wondered how I might have measured up, and at last I could only think that the young should not have to die in wars. Arthur Marwick, in *The Deluge,* reports that by the end of 1916, "Each day the newspapers carried a list of about 4,000 casualties." Britain lost, as Marwick puts it, "the tithe of a generation." About 745,000 of the nation's younger men were killed, or about nine percent of all men under forty-five. That does not include some number of the 1.6 million wounded who were seriously mutilated. ¶Grievous as all that may be, I may in my dream have used war and loss to mask other matters that I didn't want to think about. The woman in the dream may, after all, be myself, worrying about my children. I want to believe that I thought and worried about them equally, but perhaps I was thinking in particular of my older daughter; at time of the dream, I had not seen her for nine years. Asleep or awake, I sometimes can't think about that. Perhaps, in a dream rhetoric, I found a way to wrap my story inside another story. ¶One other circumstance may help to account for the events of the first two dream segments. Shortly before our trip to Mexico City, a book I wrote, called *Hunting Lieutenant Chadbourne,* was published. I had found some of the young lieutenant's letters, and then I had spent three or four years, pretty much obsessed, trying to learn about his life and his death. He was twenty-two when he was killed on May 9, 1846, at the Battle of Resaca de la Palma at the very beginning of the United States' war with Mexico. On the day before the dream (the same day I took late lunch at the "almost pub"), I had spent the morning walking to and through Chapultepec Park. There I came upon the great memorial to Mexico's soldiers who fell in the same war. I was jolted into grief, partly because of my own selfish concerns. Perhaps it was because I had been immersed in learning about a young man on the other side. Perhaps it was because the memorial stunned me into knowledge, once again, that young men should not have to die in old men's wars. ¶I cannot make sense of the dream's third segment except to say that I was still shaken when I woke by a profound sense of loss and hurt. I do not know what to make of the mustard. Perhaps the war setting of the first two segments somehow triggered some lost notion of mustard gas. That, of course, makes no sense at all. Why would she be forlorn at the loss of a vile weapon? Perhaps the parable of the mustard seed, with its hope of something momentous, somehow twined itself in there somewhere. I do remember watching her once when she was about five and was at play on the campus across the street from our house. She saw a bird that appeared to be a little lame, hobbling along on the ground. I saw her run toward the bird, her arms stretched out in front of her to help the bird. As she neared, the bird half-flew, half-hopped away. The two of them repeated their actions three or four times. Afterward, she told me that she wanted to help, but couldn't catch the little bird. ¶My children are not gone. All three are alive, and they prosper tolerably. All are in other lives. All are gone as I knew them in dear moments of our past. I have not been able to keep them. I have not been able to dig out what may be buried there.

What Is Lost (III)

What I think I see already may have disappeared, transposed—like Rome's power—to
Byzantium, and the light on this summer
morning no more than a filter for my mis-
perception, a screen.

—Nicholas Christopher

Much, of course, remains in the personal archives that each of us car-
ries around, filed, fingered, refiled, kept, whether verifiable or created,
remembered or misremembered. Much, however, is gone and oftener
than not irretrievable. Much is lost that I know is lost. Much is lost
that I never knew. Much is lost that I went off and left. Much is lost
that I chose not to see. ¶Now, from the dream I have just mentioned,
I should add another category. Much is lost that I have edited and
repressed, or repressed by editing, or edited by repressing. ¶And then
I should add another category of losses. In that dream of children, I
was somehow there, watching, but I was not present, I was not an
actor. ¶Many have remarked that the *I* is missing from most English
sentences. If at an elegant party I should sip and say, "This wine is very
nice," the original that I have already edited is something like, "I *think*
this wine is very nice." As Walker Gibson has noted, the unexpressed
subject of every English sentence is *I,* but, for a variety of reasons, we
conventionally transform most sentences from speaker/author-present
sentences to speaker/author-absent sentences. In most of the writing
that we do—in newspapers, magazines, term papers, memos, reports,
manuals, textbooks, case histories, laboratory reports—we have elimi-
nated signs of authorship. ¶Then it's all the more difficult to find each
utterance's archives. When I say or write something, I am already gone,
and neither I nor the other out there can find me, except, perhaps, in
pieces. When another speaks or writes, I cannot find him or her, except,
perhaps, in pieces. I search to account for Keats' "Ode on a Grecian

Urn," and I get some clues from his letters and from what's known about his life, but despite excellent and engaging and compelling studies of his work, I cannot at last fit the last two lines to the poem. The personal history before each discourse of utterance, the autobiography that accompanies each discourse or utterance and holds its sources, is gone.

Fragments of a Personal Canon

Something has always already been filling our experience before we have stopped to notice and to name it. We are always seeing where we are through where we were, where we were through where we are. When we study a rhetoric, our own or some other, we are always studying it through a rhetoric we have already long since inhabited. Long before any one of us knows that there are canons, literary or otherwise, each of us already has a sacred personal canon. However, when we come to survey the sources, teaching, and faculties that we like to suppose have been the chief guides of our thought and behavior, we characteristically miss this sacred personal canon. We miss it because we can't see it, at least not always and at least not in its entirety. Because we usually can't see it, and can never see it in its entirety, we don't know that it is sacred or that it is personal, though not exclusively so, and we don't know that it has the shape, character, and power of a canon. ¶I cannot identify my own sacred personal canon, let alone describe another's. For each of us, it is a set of texts of extraordinary diversity. Kilroy graffiti form a text, and chapters in a movie serial, and Burma Shave signs along the highway. Our canon, I expect, has usually been pretty well gathered by age twelve, or before the onset of the ravages and enticements of adolescence, but we can't see all of it: some we noticed, but then forgot; those we remember, we have usually misremembered. If we could see it all, it would loom as large and as plain as what some like to call the Great Tradition or the Great Books. ¶This set of texts is sacred because long before we know it exists, it has already become part of the nature of things. It teaches us how to view the world and what expectations of it to hold. It teaches us spatial and temporal relationships, and how to view ourselves in the world. It teaches us how to use language and what expectations of that to hold. This canon is sacred: even as we gather it, it becomes and will ever after remain our guide and our antagonist, our standard for measuring good and bad, right or wrong, its power never easily shaken even when we learn more and better. It informs us as we think, speak, and write the quaint novels, the odd autobiographies, the acknowledged and unacknowledged histories that are our lives, and it notifies us when we fail. I'll go on to suggest even, that all those other sources, teachings, and faculties—genetic disposition, Jungian image, the subconscious, the unconscious, judgment, reason, wit, family history, socioeconomic circumstance—can be rendered null before the quiet strength of this canon. It begins early and surrounds us. The analyst, for example, who looks chiefly to the unconscious as a source of understanding is already late in our chronology. The sacred canon is seldom a source of altogether sure wisdom, and sometimes not even of sanity. Because it takes shape within as expectations without experiences, many of us find the world and ourselves are forever disconsonant with our own canonical expectations. ¶I call this canon personal because it grows in and with our largely accidental experiences, more often by meander than by plan. I suppose that it cannot be deemed exclusively personal, since much that we experience we encounter with others. Still, no matter how many of us may look at the same set of texts, no two of us will see the same canon, because each of us is already looking out through a canon still being formed, though some apparently close early. ¶This canon is a common source, perhaps the commonest source of our instruction in some culture or set of cultures. Source of our scripture, belief, liturgy, and practice, it is our real, though usually unacknowledged, canon. Few if any of us will teach this canon because we generally are both unable and unwilling: we don't know it except in fragments, and we won't acknowledge it because when we do unearth some of our canonical sources, we find that many are quite trivial. Yet, our beliefs, values, critical judgments, ways of thinking rise among these fragments, and those of us who are school teachers will, it seems clear, teach our canons whether or not we know and acknowledge them. We look at any canon through some canon. ¶If I want to understand even a little how and why I came to see, to think, to behave, to say as I have done,

I must examine the canon I look through. If I want to understand even a little how and why I have taught as I have done, or how, if at all, I may account for myself, I must examine the canon I look through. ¶I can't examine that canon. I can't find it. I know only some fragments of it. Most of it is irretrievable. I know that billboards and store windows and movie posters and cereal boxes were among my canonical texts, but they are gone. Some early school texts are there, but I couldn't begin to identify them. Some popular songs, country songs, and honky-tonk songs got into my mind and stayed. I still sing "Honky-Tonk Angel," "The Great Speckled Bird," "The Crash on the Highway," and "The Wabash Cannonball" when I'm alone in my office. War stories from World War II are there. I heard one story from my father at the end of the war that seemed to define heroism and brotherhood. A man from our old community was killed during a bombing raid over Europe. A senior sergeant, he stayed aboard a crippled B-17 after the rest of the crew had bailed out, working on the jammed hatch of the ball turret where a young gunner was still trapped, working, working as they went down together. President Reagan told essentially the same story to a group of reporters some forty years later. Neither they nor I thought to wonder how anyone might have known what the sergeant was doing if he and the young gunner died, if all the rest had bailed out, if no one was left alive to tell their story. ¶No matter. The story defined heroism and brotherhood, I thought, and I have always failed on both accounts. ¶At any rate, war stories, usually apocryphal, are in my canon. So are God knows how many more movies, western novels, western pulp magazines, and books that I would want to count if I could remember them. ¶And hymns are there. Sermons probably got inside my head early, too, but I've lost all the words except *sin, hellfire,* and *damnation.* Hymns are another matter, though: they were often repeated, and the music helped keep them in my head. They still bedevil me. I sing them when I'm alone in my office and sometimes when I work in the yard. Indeed, I'm convinced that they form an important part of my personal canon, the more so because they were frequently repeated texts in my little world that had relatively few competing texts. ¶I lived as a boy with my family in a small rural community. We had

And hymns are there. Sermons p[...]

early, too, but I've lost all the w[...]

<u>damnation</u>. Hymns are another matter[...]

repeated, and the music helped keep[...]

bedevil me. I sing them when I'm al[...]

when I work in the yard. Indeed, I'[...]

important part of my personal canon[...]

were frequently-repeated texts in m[...]

relatively few competing texts.

I lived as a boy with my famil[...]

We had no radio until 1938, when I [...]

altogether reliable, and I never fu[...]

I did not regularly see newspapers [...]

and we ~~have~~ had moved to the big city. [...]

didn't routinely see magazines unti[...]

theater in the little town where we[...]

[...]en, and I didn't always have a di[...]

no radio until 1938, when I was nine years old. It wasn't altogether reliable, and I never fully developed the radio habit. I did not regularly see newspapers until 1941, when I was twelve and we had moved to the big city. For scarcity of money, I didn't routinely see magazines until later. There was a movie theater in the little town where we lived, but it wasn't always open, and I didn't always have a dime. I didn't regularly see movies until 1942, when I was thirteen. My early life was not, you might say, cluttered with diverse texts. ¶But there were always hymns. My mother and father were devout Baptists. They went to church three times a week—for two regular services on Sunday and for prayer meeting on Wednesday evening. When they went to church, I went with them, from necessity, not piety. My memories of church began at least by the time I was five years old. By the time I was twelve, my parents would sometimes let me stay at home to do my homework instead of going to Wednesday prayer meeting. ¶I'll take that eight-year period, then, as a sample. My family went to church unless there was dire illness. A year would have 156 church attendance possibilities (3 a week for 52 weeks). I'll reduce that to 150 to allow for our absences, and there wouldn't have been that many. In 8 years, then, I'd have been to church about 1,200 times. The typical pattern of service had three hymns early and one hymn at the end (the invitational hymn), for a total of four, or about 4,800 hymn opportunities in the eight-year period. ¶Of course, I did not hear or sing 4,800 different hymns. Of the hymns available in the hymnals of that small rural church, I reckon now that there were probably not more than about one hundred that were in standard, frequent use. The preacher would not have known or liked some of the others. The choir director would not have known or liked some. I'd guess that the pianist probably couldn't handle just any hymn. The congregation wouldn't have gotten its spirits up for just any hymn. ¶Perhaps one hundred standard hymns, then, and about 4,800 chances to hear them. Frequent repetition would occur. The repetition worked: many of them have stayed in my head. ¶What did I learn from this canon? What did I learn from these repetitions that still continue as I sing (badly) in my office or in the yard or in the shower? The gentler hymns don't seem to have stayed with me. For just about all of my adult life, I have supposed that I learned hard, bleak, and lonesome lessons. I have seldom heeded most of these lessons, but they are always there in my mind as standards against which I must inevitably be found lacking. ¶I think I learned that I should always be *vigilant* and *hard-working,* though that has not been the case. I learned that I should

> Rescue the perishing, care for the dying,
> Snatch them in pity from sin and the grave;
> Weep o'er the erring one, lift up the fallen,
> Tell them of Jesus, the mighty to save.

And I think I learned that I should

> Work, for the night is coming, work thro' the morning hours;
> Work while the dew is sparkling, work mid springing flow'rs;
> Work, when the days grow brighter, work in the glowing sun;
> Work, for the night is coming, when man's work is done.

I think I learned that I should always be militant and brave, though I have seldom been either. I learned that I should

> Bear the news to ev'ry land, climb the steeps and cross the waves;
> Onward! 'tis our Lord's command: Jesus saves, Jesus saves.

And I think that I was told, repeatedly, that I should

> Yield not to temptation, for yielding is sin,
> Each vict'ry will help you some other to win;
> Fight manfully onward, dark passions subdue,
> Look ever to Jesus, He'll carry you through.

I should have learned to fight bravely, I guess, for I heard such admonitions often:

Stand up, stand up for Jesus, ye soldiers of the cross;
Lift high his royal banner, it must not suffer loss;
From vict'ry until vict'ry His army shall lead,
Till ev'ry foe is vanquished and Christ is Lord indeed.

I think I learned that I should be *submissive,* though I haven't always been, because of my own, well-demonstrated *inadequacy, sin,* and *guilt:*

Guide me, O thou great Jehovah,
Pilgrim through this barren land;
I am weak, but thou art mighty;
Hold me with thy powerful hand;
Bread of heaven, bread of heaven,
Feed me till I want no more.

And there was this, always unmistakably in mind:

Rock of Ages, cleft for me,
Let me hide myself in thee;
Let the water and the blood,
From thy riven side which flowed,
Be of sin the double cure,
Cleanse me from its guilt and power.

And this, heard often in church and especially at funerals, stayed with me:

What a Friend we have in Jesus,
All our sins and griefs to bear!

And so did this:

When other helpers fail, and comforts flee,
Help of the helpless, O abide with me.

And especially this:

> There is a fountain filled with blood,
> Drawn from Immanuel's veins;
> And sinners, plunged beneath that flood,
> Lose all their guilty stains.
> The dying thief rejoiced to see
> That fountain in his day;
> And there may I, though vile as he,
> Wash all my sins away.

When I look back, I believe I learned very well to know that I am *inadequate,* full of *sin* and *guilt,* but I never entirely learned to be *submissive.* To be sure, my mind has held some hymns of hope:

> When the trumpet of the Lord shall sound and time shall be no more,
> And the morning breaks eternal, bright and fair;
> When the saved of earth shall gather over on the other shore,
> And the roll is called up yonder, I'll be there.

But, it has always seemed to me, even where some signs of hope appeared, they were undercut by signs of weariness, bleak signs of longing and loss. One hymn invites us to "gather at the river," but its last stanza reminds us that we're not yet there:

> Soon we'll reach the shining river,
> Soon our pilgrimage will cease;
> Soon our happy hearts will quiver
> With the melody of peace.

Even when we reach sweet Beulah land, we're still not there:

> O Beulah land, sweet Beulah land,
> As on thy highest mount I stand,

I look away across the sea,
Where mansions are prepared for me,
And view the shining glory shore,
My heav'n, my home for evermore.

These are fragments of what would be only one small chapter of my personal canon. If I were to look through other hymnals, I'd probably find other hymns that have stayed in my mind. I would find many that I do not recollect at all, and I would not find some that I remember. If I found every hymn that I once heard sung, and sang myself, I still wouldn't be able to answer questions that nag at me: How was it that I came to do all the things that I have done? How was it that I came to be whoever I turned out to be? ¶I would learn a little of course, perhaps even more than a little, but when I set out to determine what I learned from these repetitions that still continue as I sing in my office or in the yard or in the shower, I'm trying to examine a canon that developed *then* through the canons and rhetoric that have developed *since*. ¶I can't find this little section of my personal canon, or, were I to find it, know it. I can't teach this canon, but of course I do. The texts of a personal canon teach first lessons that cannot be readily escaped. The personal canon is the site of the soul's first shaping. First lessons are durable even if we learn better. School teachers, though, are fortunate, or may be. They are situated where they can, if they will, continue going to school. If we do, we may come to know of our own first lessons, the texts of our own personal canons, to hold and to cherish some, to teach them knowingly, and to free ourselves of others.

Missing Persons

You can't
Lie down without turning your back
On someone.

—James Galvan

I ask myself: If I exhibit Behavior A or say Sentence A, do I know why? If I know why, will that explain why I've done Behavior A or said Sentence A instead of doing Behavior B or saying Sentence B? ¶In answer, I tell myself that I have a few reasonably good ideas but that most are pretty vague. I can't ever convince myself that I'm certain because too much is missing from my archives. Scraps, paragraphs, pages, whole chapters are missing from the autobiography I'm always thinking inside my head. I don't have all of the evidence. ¶I tell myself I have a reasonably accurate recollection and a reasonably good sense of the people who have in some way or another entered and exited my life, since I started paying attention. But whom have I missed from that time? And how do I know that I was indeed paying attention yesterday? I have to come into consciousness all over again just about every day. And whom have I missed from before the time when I like to imagine that I started paying attention? ¶I tell myself that if I could get people all in mind, identified, sorted, lined up so that I could see all of them, then I'd have better archives, a better set of evidences for myself. I go looking. Where shall I look? Probably anywhere. We're all lost. ¶Where shall I look? I go back to that brief time before I like to think I began remembering, and even then I remember two or three quick images. I remember a little red metal race car that I got for Christmas in Seymour. It had a battery that made the headlights shine, and my father used it for a flashlight when he was fixing the car somewhere on the way to Grandma and Grandpa Durham's farm. I remember a hobo at our back door in Seymour. I think my mother gave him food. That summer night, I was sleeping on a pallet by the open back door to catch the little breeze, and I had a nightmare, apparently. Someone awful came to the door, and I must have cried out. My father came and eased my fear. "Don't worry," he said. "If someone comes to get you, I'll pee on him." That seemed enough. I think I saw other hobos, but that wasn't unusual. David Baker says in his poem, "Still Life With Jacket,"

> In nineteen thirty-four, the poor were
> everywhere migrating. They wanted,
> if not a living, at least some food.
> They found dust and trouble. Little work.

One other image has stayed with me, though I didn't have any idea then, and little now, of its significance. In Seymour in 1934, I remember, I once saw a strange thing. My mother, father, brother, and I lived in half of a house. I think it was a regular house; I don't much think we knew about duplexes then and there. A young couple lived in the other side. I don't remember the man at all. The young woman, I think, was pretty. She may have been beautiful. How was I to know? I was playing on the front porch in the shade—in the summer, Seymour often has the highest temperature in Texas. I passed by the front window of the other side of the house, where the young couple lived. The window was open wide, and the shade had been raised. The young woman was, I guess, asleep on a bed by the window, and I could see her plainly. I expect she was trying to catch the breeze, too, if there was any. I didn't know then what I was seeing, what it was she was wearing. Later, when I learned to read and to study the Montgomery Ward catalog, I sort of figured it out: she was wearing a black brassiere and black panties. I didn't know that then, but I did know that something strange had happened, that I probably shouldn't have been there, that I probably shouldn't have seen her. She stayed in my mind. ¶Where shall I look to find who counted? I go back to the five years we lived in Jayton, when I began to notice and to remember a little more surely, and I want to say that everyone counts, but then I ask myself, "Who taught me, who changed me, who counted directly to me?" ¶Two preachers? Surely. Brother Ogletree and Brother Hinson. I assumed then that *brother* was their proper title, if not actually part of their names. They "saved" me while filling me with sin, if I wasn't already full. Friends? Jimmy Matthews and Don Jones are still in my mind. Teachers? Yes: Mamie Morris Murphy, my first-grade teacher, who got married and then was Mamie Morris Murphy Fowler; Fannie Beth Rice, my second-grade teacher, who died young, as I would learn later; Sue Kinney with the beautiful auburn hair, my third-grade teacher and the youngest of the lot, whom I loved deeply if not passionately, though I would have done that, too, if I'd known how; Mrs. Check Jay (real first name— Cherokee), my fourth grade teacher and widow of one of the town's founders. Mr. Holley, the only Sunday School teacher I remember and the town drayman? Yes. I don't know anything consciously now about his Sunday teaching, and I don't know whether or not any of it got in at some other level. I do remember riding with him once in a while on his wagon. He took the mail from the depot to the post office every day. He delivered lumber for the Callicoate lumber yard. He carried the town's stuff. Who else? I probably should include Buck Jones, Tom Mix, Hopalong Cassidy, and Ken Maynard from down at the picture show, and Jack, Doc, and Reggie, whom I heard in "I Love a Mystery" whenever we had a radio, and the gunfighters, villains, cowboys, and ladies that I read about when my parents could afford to buy a copy of *Ranch Romances*. Who else? Who else, indeed? ¶Some are real, and stay with me, even if I can't decipher what they may have taught me—John Hunt, R. L. Anderson, and George Weatherly, my friends through high school; Maltie Mae Solon and Reta Oglesby, teachers from high school; the soldiers, sailors, mariners, and fliers of World War II, all superior beings, while I was an embarrassed inferior for not being with them. Some farm families, I'm told, came into Jayton once in a while on Saturdays for groceries, more often on Sundays for church. I don't think I knew any of them. I wish I had, for they are gone now. Forty years after we left Jayton, I asked the new young Baptist preacher there if many people from out in the country came in for church. ¶"A few do," he said, "from the north part of the country." ¶I asked why there were none from the south part of the county. ¶"There's no one out there," he said. ¶I wish I had known them and kept their names, but they died or moved on, and now they are lost to me. ¶Lost to me, too, and never known, are the girls and women I began to think about a lot as the war went on—well, perhaps not all of them. Of course, I can't claim that what I did can rightly be called thinking. I had no idea what one did with what or with whom. ¶Some of the others from that time were real, too, and they stayed with me for a long time, though I made them up in the first place and probably wouldn't have liked them much if I had known them. I thought Arturo Toscanini must be wonderful for introducing me to what I thought of as "classical music." I didn't learn until long after that what he introduced me to was a fairly narrow repertoire of musical pieces that he thought it was best for me and others to hear. I thought Cecil B. DeMille must be wonderful because on the radio on Monday nights he presented Lux Radio Theater, especially "Wuthering Heights." I didn't catch on until later that what I heard one night was a reduction of a reduction, a radio program made from a movie made from the novel. Even so, when I later read the book and saw the movie with Laurence Olivier and Merle Oberson, neither quite created the chill and wonder I felt that Monday night. ¶Most of the others who were real in that time, but made up in my mind, were baseball players: Honus Wagner, Christy Mathewson, Ty Cobb, Babe Ruth, Walter Johnson, Paul Waner, Lou Gehrig, Bobby Feller, Luke Appling, Dizzy Dean, Johnny Van Der Meer, and especially my great favorites, Charley Gehringer and Joe Dimaggio. Some of them were probably louts and drunks, but I thought they must be gentleman and pure. I made and eventually lost many baseball scrapbooks. Who else is lost? ¶Many of the other missing persons from that time were never real from the beginning, and just here, much later, I encountered what remains a great mystery to me: Which hard and primary lessons did I actually learn from stories, fantasies? While I thought I was being a tolerably decent person, had I learned much that was altogether false, but later hard to surrender? I remember some of them: from books, Ivanhoe, Dr. Doolittle, Sherlock Holmes, the Scarlet Pimpernel, the three wonderful brothers Geste; from movies, Leslie Howard, Ronald Colman, Zorro, and the rest; from comic strips and comic books, the Blackhawks, the Phantom, Captain Easy and Wash Tubbs, Scorchy

Smith, Oakey Doakes, Tailspin Tommy, Smilin' Jack, Buck Rogers, Flash Gordon, the Shadow, what people would call the "scantily-clad women" of *Wings Comics,* and then the Dragon Lady and Miss Burma and Miss Lace from Milt Caniff, and Sheena of the Jungle (I never paid a lot of attention to her stories, but she was certainly interesting to see). If not well, I remember these, but whom have I forgotten? Where did I learn those hard and primary lessons that later I found so difficult to understand, to keep, or to shed? Was I constructed from the lumber, bolts, and nails of a world that never was? Such questions, I guess, are selfish and perhaps despondent, with no high expectation that a happy ending will make all in time for me to know it. I examine myself; perhaps I also fear to examine myself. ¶ Still, Cleckler Street, where my family lived in the early 1940s, was mostly sweet, and the shade was blue under the arching trees and across our house. That was a long time ago. The speaker in Jo McDougall's poem, "I'll Be Seeing You," says,

> World War II is slipping away, I can feel it.
> Its officers are gray.
> Their wives who danced at the USO
> are gray, too.
> Veterans forget their stories. Some lands they fought in
> have new names, and Linda Venetti
> who deserted the husband who raised cows
> to run off with an officer
> has come home to look after her mother
> and work the McDonald's morning shift.
> William Holden is dead,
> and my mother, who knew all the words
> to "When the Lights Go On Again All Over the World."

Then where shall I look to find all of those who somehow counted, even if I didn't know it at the time? During the years just after the war, I was sometimes frantic, sometimes hungry; I was working mostly full time in a laboratory and going to college, and a good part of that time,

I think, was barely conscious. Probably there is far more in those years than I have remembered and a little more than I want to think about. Perhaps I had already learned all those hard and primary lessons from other people, all the lessons I would learn. Sometimes I have thought so, those lessons that later were difficult to understand, to keep, or to shed. Right now I don't think so. ¶I go looking, and find no names, but another mystery. In 1951, I went involuntarily to Germany with the 57th Medium Tank Battalion, part of the 2nd Armored Division. We were stationed outside Mannheim, ten or twelve miles from Heidelberg. According to my duty, I complained almost all of the time, but the truth is that some of my time there was pleasant enough. I was young, and, when I left the military post, free of responsibility. On weekends, three-day passes, and leaves, I could walk and look as much as I pleased, and what I saw delighted me—to one who had never before left Texas, the towns were quaint and picturesque, the forests deep and lovely, the hills and river valleys beautiful, as they would be still. I had already been startled to discover that I was the alien; now I was pleased to know that I was invisible and could ramble as I wished. ¶If I was delighted, I was also puzzled and troubled, drawn toward a mystery that I sensed only in the vaguest way, a mystery that has deepened since, while my understanding of it still remains inchoate after these forty-five years. Most of what I saw then, when I was young, I didn't understand. In Heidelberg, I didn't know what the public buildings were, or why the castle was situated just so on the hill above the town, or how a twenty-year-old building could shoulder up against one built five centuries ago—in West Texas, few buildings of any kind are as much as a century old. In Mannheim, I saw buildings everywhere that had been damaged or destroyed by bombs, but I assumed then that all of these bombs had accidentally strayed from their military and industrial targets. I didn't learn until much later that we had deliberately bombed civilians, their homes, their places of work. ¶What has remained a mystery to me, certainly never unique to me alone, I can say simply enough: Why was I drawn to learn and understand about Nazi Germany? Everything about Germany's recent presence in my mind was hateful. In 1951 and 1952, I was officially a member of an Army of

Occupation, therefore officially an enemy of Germany. Perhaps I was caught up, as most of us were caught up, in wondering how all of the events, disasters, and tragedies of the Nazi rise, rule, and fall could have happened. And if I was caught up in this mystery and troubled by it, then a corollary question emerges: Why didn't I set out to study Nazi Germany systematically rather than spasmodically? ¶In the years since, I've had time to consider my original question, but never time enough to answer it, except partially. I can account in some small way for the attraction Germany has had for me, and I reckon that is already apparent. For a long time, I have been disturbed and entranced and perhaps obsessed—though that last characteristic probably ought to be ascribed by another rather than proclaimed of oneself—by the difficulty, impossibility, of knowing very much of anything with certainty. I know what kind of pipe tobacco I want to smoke, and I know which cheap white wine I want to drink, but after that things get chancy. When I ask to know the proper names of our weeds, given regional and colloquial variations, few agree. I haven't found the Polar community, or Oriana, and no one can tell me the exact site of the Duck Creek school. I have no recollection at all of some places, things, and events that I should have noticed well and remembered. Those that I do remember I have often, if not always, misremembered in part or altogether. Many of the archives I've searched for are gone because they never existed. Over the years, I think that Germany came to be a locus for mystery, came to localize and to embody the impossibility of knowing much for certain. Over the years, I came to think that I would never know all that intrigued me—the dark forests, the old tales, the castles, the towns—and more, could not know them. ¶I'm even less certain about answering my second question: Why didn't I study systematically? Preoccupation with other matters gives a partial answer. Indolence gives another. ¶Perhaps I have been afraid of what I would learn, about myself, about ourselves. ¶I'd just as soon not have to acknowledge, even to myself, that a culture both hateful and attractive, at least in its non-political, non-militaristic manifestations, if such exist, would also awaken in me a seldom dormant prurient response. I think that is despicable, but probably not the only or most despicable feature of my character. Still, I find myself wondering what the relationship was between Hitler and Geli Raubal, the daughter of his half-sister. In *The Hitler File,* Frederic V. Grunfeld says that she was his mistress and that she, not Eva Braun, was "the one great love of Hitler's life." Grunfeld also records a twice-removed story—which, I guess, makes this at least a thrice-removed story—that she said her uncle was a monster: "No one can imagine what he expects me to do for him." Hitler was reported to have made a series of pornographic drawings of her in "positions and close ups for which any professional model would refuse to pose." Geli Raubal killed herself in 1931. And how can I not be sickened by myself when I am titillated, mildly, by accounts of various German nudist cults, even when I know, as Wilfried van der Will puts it in his discussion contained in his and Brandon Taylor's *The Nazification of Art,* that "the sheen of the bodies of Fascist nudes was that of the pretension to master-race status which carried a death warrant for those who could not satisfy the legally and bureaucratically enshrined criteria of racial conformity"? And how can I tolerate my own pleasure in nude painting of the Nazi era—Klein's *The Repose,* for example, or Engelhards' *Bathing in a Mountain Lake,* or Hilz's *Peasant Venus?* ¶Do you imagine that I tell my blackest secrets? I haven't nerve for that. I tell only those that are dingy. ¶And that won't do. If I am to know what I have held and what I have lost, I must be honest, and I must try to get everything down right. ¶I can't. Not yet. ¶Perhaps, if I studied my interest in Nazi Germany, I might have learned truths close to ourselves at the end of the twentieth century. "Death has no sting for us," Himmler said, because "individuals die, while the Volk lives on." How, exactly, I wonder, does that differ from the arguments advanced by composition theorists in the last ten to fifteen years that all writing assignments, including personal essays, should be done collaboratively? In what way, I wonder, is the Nazi propagandistic hope for an "organic community" different from the frequent contemporary complaint against "selfish individualism"? And does that hope have room in it for the current social constructionist contention that writing is always created by the group, not by the privileged author? And what shall I make of the argument made by Zygmunt Bauman and others that the Holocaust was a product, not of failure, but of modernity? Every ingredient of the Holocaust, Bauman says,

> ... was normal; 'normal' not in the sense familiar, of one more specimen in a large class of phenomena long ago described in full, explained and accommodated (on the contrary, the experience of the Holocaust was new and unfamiliar), but in the sense of being fully in keeping with everything we know about our civilization, its guiding spirit, its priorities, its immanent vision of the world—and of the proper ways to pursue human happiness together with a perfect society.

Paul Hilberg concluded that "the machinery of destruction, then, was structurally no different from organized German society as a whole. The machinery of destruction was the organized community in one of its special roles." Bauman goes on to add that

> Modern civilization was not the Holocaust's *sufficient* condition; it was however, most certainly its *necessary* condition. Without it, the Holocaust would be unthinkable. It was the rational world of modern civilization that made the Holocaust thinkable.

The technological achievement of an industrial society and the organizational achievement of a bureaucratic society, the Holocaust, Bauman proposes, "did not clash at any stage with the rational pursuit of efficient, optimal goal-implementation," and both the institutions responsible for the Holocaust and the people "whose actions they institutionalized did not deviate either from established standards of normality." ¶Ah well, I came upon an obsession with Nazi Germany by the happenstance of an involuntary assignment, and I never pursued any study systematically. I am haunted by what I don't know. ¶I tell myself that if I could get people all in mind, identified, sorted, lined up so that I could see all of them, then I'd have better archives, a better set of evidences for myself and for the world. ¶I go looking. Where shall I look? Probably anywhere. I won't find those that I have lost. ¶I do find some names and some mysteries. ¶From time to time when I was a young man, less often later, not at all now (and besides, she is dead), I created marvelous fictions featuring a variety of sexual encounters with one of my aunts, in which she, the older woman, initiated me, the boy, into all kinds of exciting mysteries. She was not, however, the only star of my fantasies. Oftener than not, I was, or sometimes I imagined myself to be, the wise and thoughtful older lover initiating some beautiful girl to wonders. No, not oftener than not: I was always the star, though in most fantasies I wanted to believe that I was co-star with equals. Fantasies were frequent. Scenarios often changed. Indeed, I sometimes couldn't imagine myself as far along as the best part because I took so long deciding upon which delicious scenario that my mind wandered, or I fell asleep. ¶I was, in those former years, frequently feverish. ¶I have wondered, over and over, why this was so. It is another mystery that I can't entirely understand, though I believe I do understand some of the commonplace explanations, and I know that I am commonplace. ¶My own motives are often no clearer to me than they may sometimes be to others, but I don't believe that I have ever wanted power over a beautiful woman, though I know that it may sometimes have looked otherwise to another. I don't believe that I have ever wanted to own a beautiful woman as a commodity, though another may have interpreted my behavior as if I had done so. I go looking and find some names and some mysteries. ¶I thought that I was special, rare, liberated from old male protocols and expectations, wanting only a happy and eager partner, or a series of them. I turned out to be, at best, simply an ordinary male, at best an ordinary product of my time and culture. Why did I let myself succumb to the little myths of maleness? Who taught me? Why didn't I know better? My ways of imagining women turned out to be, at best, ordinary, silly, expectable, perhaps sometimes monstrous. I was educated by ordinary teachers, indoctrinated in canons and gospels that I should have questioned from the outset. I know some of them, but not all. ¶Still, they were beautiful, warm, and exciting, those women in my mind, and many have stayed in my mind, though I lost many. One was from

The American Magazine, perhaps in 1943, perhaps in 1944. In those days, the magazine published in each issue what was what was called a "book-length mystery." The image was an illustration of one such story. It shows a beautiful young woman who has just crawled through a window and put one leg over the back of a sofa in front of the window. The action has pulled her skirt well up her thigh. God, she was beautiful. I can call her back now. In 1943 or maybe 1944, that was about as exciting as it gets, and it is still. ¶The other image was on the cover of *Life,* maybe 1944, or early 1945. The whole issue was devoted to showing what was waiting in the country "when the boys come home." The photograph shows a car, its driver's side to the viewer, the driver's door standing open. In the passenger seat, a beautiful young woman with long blonde hair sits, her left arm over the driver's seat. She is looking toward the viewer, or toward the "boy" who will come home, and she has half-turned, expectantly. Turning has pulled her skirt up to show maybe three or four inches of her thighs. God, she was beautiful. I had never seen anything as sexy. I can call her back now. ¶And what about Helen and Gloria and Rachel and Ruth and Peggy? They starred with me in wonderful movies of the mind. What about all of the pin-ups of World War II? They've mostly disappeared, unless one is willing to hunt through newspaper archives of the time. What about Maria and Joyce and Margaret, especially Margaret, and Ann and Joan and Billy and Betsy and Susan and Linda and Nancy and Leslie and Sarah? Once I wrote wonderful chapters in my mind in which each was the central figure. How beautiful they all were. I can call them back now. ¶Each should be celebrated for herself, not for my longing and lust, but only I remember each as I remember each. ¶Whom have I forgotten? ¶One whom I did not forget was beautiful FJ, whose name I still cannot say in this company. She was in a special place, and she was sacred. In the sixth grade, I became her lover, always from afar, and she wrote FJ + JWC inside a heart on the cover of my textbook. We sat side by side in Mrs. Edwards' classroom, and I guess I was never again that close to her, though I loved her forever, or until I forgot, though that was temporary. I didn't know it at the time, and didn't realize until much later, but she was two years older than I was, as were almost all of my classmates. In time, when I looked back, I thought that all of them were more knowledgeable as well. Perhaps that accounts for a strange thing that happened not long ago. ¶In all the fevered and horny imaginings of my youth and even later, when I was picturing myself at one breast and then another, between these legs and then others, she never figured. She was apart, special, and I loved her purely. She was the holy one. Then one day recently, I was reading Rodney Jones's poem, "Apocalyptic Narrative," and came upon this passage:

> A physicist spoke of a new calendar he'd devised,
> Beginning after television, after the bomb. "We are,"
> He said, "so terribly junior to that God."
> When I was a boy, I loved my mother's biscuits
> And feared the dark; deep space; vengeance
> Of the desert prophets driving their vision dogs
> Until the sexual animal was treed in fire.
> "It's better," she said, pulling on lace panties
> Behind the church, "when you believe in hell."

Suddenly, as if without thought or remembrance, FJ was there, in a way she had never been before, pulling on lace panties, showing me the way. I was for a moment overwhelmed by lust, but then I put her back in her sacred place. I don't know what to make of this moment. I think I am smaller than I was before. ¶Did you suppose that I would tell all, or even mention any beautiful woman who has been real to me? I do remember the loveliest moment of all, when a woman undid her bra and lifted her breast to my lips. ¶I go looking for all the people. Where shall I look? Probably anywhere. I won't find those that I have lost. Aleda Shirley's poem, "The Best Way Out Is Always Through," ends with these lines:

> I could feel people I love who are gone
> With me still. They are not, and I can't.

Lost Pieces

Things are as I see them
In the undecided light. They will not photograph.
—Robert Farnsworth

One day in class, I read a passage from an essay aloud to the students. I expect I wanted to imagine that I was illustrating a point, if I had a point, if illustrations ever illustrate points. The term *well-heeled* occurred in the passage I read. When I finished, a young woman asked me what *well-heeled* means. I'm frequently astonished when I learn, over and over again, that young people live in their world and use its languages instead of replicating mine. ¶I told her that it meant you were doing all right financially, were maybe even a little rich, at any rate able to keep yourself in good shoes, maybe able to get new shoes every once in a while, or to get new heels for the shoes you already have. Then you are, you know, *well-heeled.* I should have told her, too, but I didn't think to do so, that being *well-heeled* is sort of at the other extreme from being *down at the heels.* You know—your heels are worn down, and you're poor, unable to get new shoes, or to fix the ones you've already got, if you have any shoes. I might have told her, too, but I didn't think of it, and if I had, I wouldn't have told her, that neither being *well-heeled* or being *down at the heels* has anything to do with being *round-heeled,* which is a presumed condition among some women that I am told young men like to think about a lot. ¶And I didn't think to tell her that being well-heeled or down at the heels or round-heeled has nothing to with being a heel. If you are a heel, you are perhaps a little more modern than if you are a cur, a scoundrel, or a cad. The term came into use in Great Britain, Canada, and this country by about 1910. I haven't heard anyone use it in a long time, but that is not because there's a shortage of heels. I gather that we adopted the term heel from our own heels. Since we mostly can't see our own heels and so don't know what they're doing, I guess we took the word to refer to treacherous fellows, who do things behind our backs while we're not looking. I wish I had thought to mention this part to the young woman. Then I could have asked her if it's possible for a woman to be a heel. ¶I am reasonably well-heeled right now and have been for some time. The shoes I wear every day are Rockport brand shoes. I have a pair that is brown and a pair that is black, and I'm still a little surprised that I have two pairs at the same time. I'm told that the brand enjoys good repute for walking shoes. That is good. I like to walk. Mine mostly keep me pretty nearly perpendicular to the little part of earth I'm on. Other brands are all around, and they're all a little snazzier and jazzier than Rockports. Nike. Reebok. Nike. Reebok. Nike. Reebok. I can't think of the other brand names. Some of them are a little scary looking to me. Some of them look like they might take command once you put them on, especially if you pump them up, as I'm told you can do. None of them look much like the shoes many of us wore in the spring and summer when I was a boy. Those were called tenny shoes. That's spelled T E N N Y. I know that they are supposed to be called tennis shoes, but that was a usage reserved for the rich, who lived somewhere sort of vaguely in the East. ¶Only a little while ago—such a short while ago, it sometimes seems—it was all different about shoes. We wore tenny shoes in the spring and summer, and what a day it was when my mother finally said I could wear them. I went off to school able to leap tall buildings or thirty feet, whichever came first. In the fall and winter, my mother insisted that I wear leather shoes for warmth, with leather soles and leather heels. I never had more than one pair at a time. Sometimes they got a little worn. You might say that I wasn't well-heeled or that I was down at the heels. ¶If I wore a hole in the sole of the shoe, we'd cut a piece of cardboard to fit, slip it inside the shoe, and I'd go on wearing it. If the hole got bigger, or if I wore the heel plumb down almost to nothing, then my father would fix my shoes. ¶One night after supper, he would get out his shoe last. That's a metal form, a single stand about two feet high. On the top there was a re-placeable form—he had two of them, a smaller one for my mother and me, a larger for himself and my brother. This replaceable form was shaped like the bottom of a shoe. He'd sit by the table where the coal-oil lamp was so that he could see. I remember watching him one time from across the room by the radio. The lamp made a halo of his hair. He slipped my shoe onto the form, upside down so that he could work on the bottom. He got out his tack hammer, the tacks, his knife, and the leather he kept for these occasions. He always seemed to know where they were; I never can find the tacks at our house. Then he measured and cut a new sole or a new heel and put a small handful of tacks in his mouth. That way, both his hands were free. The head of the tack hammer was magnetized; he would touch the hammer to his lips, and a tack would magically attach itself. Then he hammered the sole or heel onto my shoe, and I was well-shod or well-heeled. ¶The funny shoes that I see everywhere now can't be fixed that way, or at all, but that doesn't surprise me much. Nike. Reebok. Nike. Reebok. I know that some are pretty faddish and will disappear. That's all right, if a little wasteful, but then most folks don't keep leather and tacks and a tack hammer and a knife and a shoe last close by anymore. ¶I don't know what became of my father's shoe-repair gear. I wish I did. Things matter. They make good weights to hold the world down, to keep memory and history from flying away in the wind. I think my mother knew that. Long after I was fully grown, she gave me the tin Karo Syrup pitcher I had used as a boy and my greatest prize, my first ball glove, which she had kept for me. ¶I guess, too, that things hold a little identity for me. They help me to remember that I was in a place at a time, doing this, that, or the other. Without the manual typewriter that I have used for years, without my pipe, I would have no distinguishable characteristics, no identity at all. ¶I don't much think that I've made things into icons, certainly not sacred icons. In the Introduction to his *Icons of America,* Marshall Fishwick remarks that "the craving for external expression of intentional convictions … only grows as confidence in religion, economics, and politics dwindles." "Icons," he says, "objectify the deep mythological structure of reality"; they are, he says, "cultural ciphers," "admired artifacts"; they help us "to decipher, to unlock, the mystery of our attitudes and assumptions." If I listen to Claude Levi-Strauss, the things I gather about me to look at are not sacred: "All sacred things," he said in *The Savage Mind,* "must have their place. Being in their place is what makes them sacred. If taken out of their place, even in thought, the entire order of the universe would be destroyed." ¶That's too much for me, much too significant for me. I have taken things out of their places so that I can keep them. I can't recreate or call back their places. I wish I could. ¶But I do wish I could remember every single thing that ever mattered to me. Things are not sacred, not iconic, but they are, or might be, what Fishwick calls "mindmarks." Daniel Boorstin proposes, in "An American Style in Historical Monuments," that "we've raced from the past to the present so quickly that we've lost or left behind many manifestations of our endeavors and achievements." In "Historic Sites and Monuments as Icons," Christopher D. Geist remarks that, as a consequence, "for many Americans there is little contact with the past except as historic sites, monuments, museums," where someone else has interpreted—that is, created—the past for us, as I do for myself. In "History, Nostalgia, and the Criminality of Popular Culture," Alison Graham says that "to live without a history is to be nothing; to live with an invented history is, even worse, to be a joke." I'd rather not do either. ¶If I want to remember and to hold things, I am not a collector. A recent news story said that top collectibles include ornate fountain pens from before 1940, unusual pocket knives, fishing tackle from the 1940s and before, lead crystal perfume bottles from the 1920s and 1930s, electric trains, motorized bicycles and balloon-tire bicycles from the 1930s to the 1960s, plastic deco radios from the 1920s and 1930s, briar pipes, tobacco tins, and plastic models from the 1950s and 1960s. ¶I want to find and to hold things that call back some little piece of my own small history. In my office at school, and here, I'm omitting pictures, which are all around me. I have a stylized, stumpy statue of Edward the Black Prince, two fired clay Indian figures, of the kind, my friend says, that can easily be found around burial mounds in the Southeast, a horseshoe big enough for a mighty big horse, a rock whose provenance I've forgotten, the bust of an old cowboy my son gave me, a roll of red tape my wife gave me before she was my wife, to commemorate administrative work I was doing at the time, the metal sculpture of a jackass and a brass hippo that my wife found, an alabaster flying fish that my grandfather gave me, a ceramic head that my younger daughter made, the tongue sticking out, and the coffee cup she made, with "Old Fart" on the side, a lead soldier—actually a World War II airman that I thought I ought to keep—two tiny ceramic bear cubs and a single spur that my older daughter gave me, a wooden coyote, a miniature slot machine that my wife found, and many old pipes (and I know where each came from). I could not begin to list the objects at home that she has helped me gather. One is my father's razor strap, worn as much on my brother and me as by his razor. Another is a metal strap that once hung from the bottom of Grandpa Durham's wagon. Upon it there hangs a metal step that enabled a fellow to get up into the wagon. We found it in a rubbish heap on what used to be Grandpa's farm long after it no longer was. I can't list them all, but prize what I have. Probably they won't confer identity upon me, but perhaps I can be found in a glimpse alongside. Yet, even while I prize these objects, they nag at me and anger me because they remind me of the significant objects that I don't have, and they remind me, too, of the significant objects that I can never have because I don't remember what they were. ¶My wife manages such things better. Most Saturdays, not if it's desperately cold or raining hard (for there's little to see and to find then) and not if we're out of town, of course, but most Saturdays, maybe forty or forty-five or the fifty-two a year provides, we follow the same schedule. I get up early, make coffee, shower, and settle in to read the paper. By then, she'll be up. When I've finished reading, I turn to the garage sale listing in the classified ads section. I mark the garage sales that look promising in the sections of the city where she likes to hunt. Then I write the addresses on a card so that she can work out her itinerary. By the time I'm ready to go to the public library, she is ready to go, too. For special outings, we go to antique stores and flea markets, but on most Saturdays she goes the round of garage sales. ¶She doesn't ever want to miss anything. She goes to the garage sales as a way of catching up on what she may have missed or never dreamed of. She always expects to find treasures. And she does. ¶But I've lost some of the things that matter. What about the tiny jar that held an entire imagined tree? The jar wasn't much bigger than those you used to get cream in when you had coffee at the café. Cathy put a whole imagined tree in it, planted it there, with soil packed around it. The tree was a slender dead branch, forking in diverse directions, maybe thirty inches high. She cut its chief features from paper and glued them to appropriate branches. For one branch she made a leaf, for another a bird, for another a nest for the bird. I carried it from 3319 Bellaire Drive North to 2542 Stadium Drive to 3137 Stadium Drive, but I don't have it any more. What about the pipe tamper that David brought to me from Williamsburg? What about the jars of rocks that Mindy collected? What about all of the rest? Tony Hoagland's poem, "Geography," asks,

> Why did we bother to invent a god
> when every common thing
> elicits and supports a miracle,
> issues light like a command?

Fluvanna

However long you've been up there, you come down off the Caprock at Post. If you drive through town and head southeasterly on Highway 84 toward Snyder, about halfway there you come to a narrow side road that angles south. It takes you to Fluvanna. All alone, that way the rim of the Caprock runs along to the right, or west, of the narrow road. Then it curves out to meet the road. You have to go back up on the Caprock. Fluvanna sits on the edge. ¶I don't know exactly why there's an ache in me for Fluvanna, or about Fluvanna. Fluvanna doesn't know me or need me. I don't know Fluvanna. Until a few years ago, I assumed, I had never even heard of Fluvanna. I was reading microfilm copies of *The Jayton Chronicle,* a weekly newspaper in the 1930's, and learned that the Fluvanna football team had come to play the Jayton team in the fall of 1938. I was there. I was always there. My big brother played on the Jayton team. I had to go to the map to find Fluvanna and then go to see it. ¶When I had done so, I thought I owned Fluvanna. I took it in my mind to be my personal representation and *aide-memoire* of loneliness and loss. I still don't know exactly why there is an ache in me for Fluvanna, or about Fluvanna. Perhaps it's because I had allowed it to disappear, not just from my memory, but from the earth. Perhaps it's the setting, there on the edge. The Caprock is not a sacred place, I think, but I've come to think that it is the western boundary of my territory. Up on top is elsewhere. ¶When we turned south on the side road, we could see the rim of the Caprock ahead where it curved easterly. The road back up is not dangerous, and the height is not great as heights go, but the way is sudden and precipitous among jutting bluffs and great boulders, and the incline is sufficient to pull a little at our small car. Drama doesn't have to be high to excite me. ¶Once we were up on the level plain, it was only a short way to Fluvanna. It's still official—there is a post office—but it's not there. Croton isn't there. Calgary isn't there. Clairemont isn't there. Fluvanna isn't there. Except for a garage that, I think, is still a working place, there are no business-es. We looked at four abandoned shells that had been businesses, but there was nothing else except farm houses near and far. Fluvanna isn't there. ¶ Scurry County—Fluvanna is in the northwest corner—was or-ganized in 1884. The 1911 almanac reports that it stretches to 621 miles, that stock raising is the principal industry, though "diversified Farm-ing is gaining in importance," with crops in cotton, corn, milo maize, caffir corn, sorghum, broom corn, Irish and sweet potatoes, walnuts and pecans. Snyder is the county seat. "Other principal towns," the almanac says, "are Dunn, Hermleigh, and Fluvanna." The 1925 alma-nac gives a population of 875 for Fluvanna, and I learn that there is a high school. The population is still at 875 in the 1936 almanac, and I'm reminded there, too, that Fluvanna was the terminal for the Roscoe, Snyder, and Pacific Railroad, coming from the west. For a long time, they didn't seem to know how to get railroad lines up onto or down off the Caprock. One line coming from the west stopped at Benjamin. The Stamford and Northwestern coming from the east stopped at Spur. They never connected. I guess by the time they learned how to connect them, they no longer needed to. The Handbook reports five businesses and an estimated population of 300 in 1947. The 1992 Almanac tells a different story. In the account of Scurry County, Fluvanna is not men-tioned. It still shows, however, in the list of town and city populations, with a population of 180. I don't know where they found that many. Fluvanna isn't there. ¶ I expect it would seem different if I got my mail at the Fluvanna post office, but out here, or over here, where I am, it looks pretty much like Fluvanna isn't there. I wanted to see Fluvanna again, and to show it to my wife, but I don't want to be there as it was before, or as it is now, or as it will be hereafter. ¶ Still, I'm lonesome for what I never knew. I don't reckon that Fluvanna was filled with thwarted poets, artists, and leaders. I reckon that it was filled with folks, and sometimes—not always—I find myself sad that Fluvanna is gone, and longing to know who lived there, where they lived, what they did and said and thought, what stories they told. I haven't the will, the energy, or the time to go and hunt for them all, and if I did, I wouldn't find them. ¶But we ought to remember the places where we were. ¶Now I thought I had. I had been to see Fluvanna, and now had come again to show her. I thought I owned Fluvanna. I took it in my mind to be my personal representation and *aide-memoire* of loneliness and loss. ¶I was wrong. My knowledge of Fluvanna was never even up to inadequate. Others had a better claim to Fluvanna all along.¶Not long after our trip to Fluvanna, we learned that a retired colleague, a professor of theatre, had died. We had never been close friends, I guess, but she was a fresh spirit, and it had always been good to know that she was there across the campus. Her obituary in the next day's newspaper astonished me. She was born in Fluvanna. She would be buried in Fluvanna. I guess that Fluvanna did not represent loneliness and loss to her. My discovery of Fluvanna was, after all, uncomprehending, my claim to it perverse, and now I would never know the town as she had known it.

Vanished Places

This world,
This world is home. But it
will never feel like home.

—Andrew Hudgins

Often, I think if I could see all the places where I have been, or wanted to be, then I might see myself there and understand. But of course, if I could see all those places, I might not be there. The speaker in Richard Lyons's poem, "Summer Vacation," remembers Mary, a girl he knew when he was fifteen:

> I no longer think of her with the obsessiveness
> that makes memories glow
> like the iconic representation of saints.
> And Mary I'm sure doesn't think of me.
> This is the equilibrium so celebrated these days,
> a vague sort of loss airbrushes each of us
> out of any picture, leaving behind the place itself.

And if I could see the places, I wouldn't see the places. "We see the landscape," Robert Riley says, "through filters of custom and taste," and, I'll add, through a filter of failed memory. The regions we believe we know or remember are as often, or more often, perceptual as much as geographical. We—I at least—have trouble seeing and remembering. ¶Perhaps I am only a frustrated modern tourist who has not yet seen all that might be seen. Perhaps, like many or most of us, I am hoping to find, or to find again, some sacred place or even the sacred place. In "Subconscious Landscapes of the Heart," Randy Hester tells of a community development in North Carolina. In its early stages of development he found, after a series of interviews, that "lifestyle and landscape were intertwined. Daily ritual had place specificity, and the cultural dependence on places seemed more widespread than people had reported." The places that mattered most to them were not the places they said should matter, but the places mapping their daily rituals, their daily or regular comings and goings and stoppings. ¶Home may even be experienced in the vicinity of one's body, as Molly Holden's poem "Facing West," suggests:

> If there's any place in this world
> where you are welcome—
> some part that is loyal, no matter how far
> or how infinitesimally
> small—that tiny, moist place
> you keep on your own person,
> you carry it with you.

At home or homeless, placed or displaced, we live in what E. C. Relph calls a "geographical life-world," which usually remains unobtrusive, being more lived than expressed. As Eric Dardel remarks, ¶Before any choice there is this "place" which we have not chosen, where the foundations of our worldly experience and our human condition establish themselves. We can change places, move, but this is still to look for a place; we need a base to set down our Being and to realise our possibilities, a here from which to discover the world, a *there* to which to go. ¶For most of us, still, home is the sacred place. A sacred place for me would have cactus, mesquite, and sagebrush. It would be quiet, and I would feel lonely once in a while. If there were towns, they would be small towns, so small that, if the high school boys played football at all, it would be six-man football. In such towns, as Richard Shelton's poem, "The Little Towns of West Texas," says,

> All the roads go somewhere else
> and never come back.

My interests, I expect, are only self-serving. I think that if I could see all the places where I have been, or might have been, or wanted to be, then

I might see myself there and understand. I've already had my future, and I know now that many of the places I have wanted to see, I will not see. I don't think that I'll be able to walk the back roads and see the villages of England and Scotland. I doubt that I'll drive the great circle route I cut out of a *New York Times* travel section—starting in Denver, on up, wandering, through Wyoming and Montana, down Idaho and Utah, on through northern Arizona and northern New Mexico, perhaps back up to Denver. I doubt that I'll walk the paths and lanes and back roads of Maine, New Hampshire, and Vermont; see Budapest or Prague. I'm sure that I won't walk the mountains of eastern Tennessee and western North Carolina and on up the Blue Ridge. It is far too late to take my father down the Mississippi in a steamboat. I am compelled toward places, and they mystify me: I am not always able to understand when places turn out to be both extraordinary and commonplace, beautiful and ugly. ¶Some sacred places, battlefields for example, mingle sacrilege with sacrifice. Asking "What gene demands old men command young men to die?" the speaker in Philip Booth's poem "Places Without Names" meditates on places where they died: Shiloh, Passchendaele, the Argonne Forest, Bull Run, Iwo Jima, the Choisin Reservoir, Anzio, Antietam, others. Yet for most, such places are without names:

> Beyond the homebound wounded
> only women, sleepless women, know the holy names:
> bed-names, church-names, place-names buried in their
> sons' or lovers' heads. Stones without voices,
> save the incised names. Poppies, stars, and crosses:
> the poverty of history. A wealth of lives. Ours, always
> ours: their holy names, these sacrilegious places.

Many of the places I have seen, I will not see again. I won't see Rober's Cave in eastern Oklahoma. I won't walk the byways of the Neckar River valley and on around Heidelberg. I won't see Evanston again, where Cathy was in school. I won't see San Angelo again, I'd guess, and I wonder how the city looked to Mindy, my youngest daughter, when she and her family moved away. I don't expect to see the mountain in West Virginia where the road winds down five sharp switchbacks into the blue shadows of the valley. I doubt that I'll go back to Galveston, where I once spent six months in a daze. I don't much think I'll go back to State College, Pennsylvania, where for four or five years in a row I attended a summer conference. That wasn't home, and it wasn't a shrine, though I sometimes thought myself a pilgrim. Each year, I flew to Pittsburgh, rented a car, and drove through Altoona to State College. That's not what counted. Two habits that could have been formed only there counted. First, after I had presented my conference paper, I could count on three or four days of isolation in a crowd, drinking as long as I wished in the Sly Fox Lounge at what was then the Sheraton Hotel. Second, I could count on taking the special route back toward Pittsburgh. For the first fifty miles or so, from State College down to Altoona, I took the back route that the map said was closed in winter. From State College, I drove to Pine Grove Mill and on to Seven Stars and Franklinville. After that, the route gets even twistier, to Spruce Creek and Water Street, with the wonderful U-turn under the railroad and up the mountainside, on to Catherine Township, Yellow Springs, Frankstown, Geeseytown, and Altoona. ¶I won't see the Clarion Hotel in New Orleans again, or the hot tub on the roof. ¶I may pass by or through Abilene, but I don't think I'll see the city. I remember one trip in particular. We know the route well, have driven it often, though not any more. ¶We go out Interstate 20, slide by Aledo without ever seeing it, then pass by Weatherford, which we can see off to our right. After another twenty-five miles or so, we come to signs telling us that if we turn south, we can go to Stephenville, and if we turn north, we can go to Mineral Wells, but we don't do either. By and by then, about another twenty-five miles, we come to Thurber and the Smokestack Cafe. You can see the old brick smokestack from a good way off; it's left over from the time before 1920 when Thurber was a boom town of up to 20,000 souls. I expect they all had souls, but if you were counting population out in Jayton, you'd have to subtract one because the Baptists said that Mr. Boone Bilberry didn't have a soul. He did get fuzzy around the edges sometimes, and sometimes disappeared altogether. Mr. Bilberry drank a little. ¶Pretty soon after Thurber, you can see the escarpment that runs north and south down that part of the state. It's known locally as Ranger Hill, but you go up the same slope, altogether a change of about 500 feet in elevation, to the north at Albany and to the south at Brownwood. Once up on top, you go quickly past Ranger and Eastland and Cisco. The very first Hilton Hotel was in Cisco. Pretty soon after that you come to Putname, a little town that died when they built Interstate 20 right through the middle of it, and to Baird, and to Clyde, and then you're there. Interstate 20 runs along the north edge of the city, but we get off at the loop that takes us around to the south. Eventually, an exit sign indicates that we've come to South 14th street. If you turn right there, you're on Highway 227, headed for San Angelo. If you turn left, or back into the city, you're on 14th Street. We go that way for a few blocks until it's time to turn left on Albany Street, and then we're really there. ¶We went to see Mindy and Bin and their children, Andrew, who is four and a half, and Kate, who is one and a half. Mindy is my youngest daughter. Bin is her husband. Andrew and Kate are our grandchildren. At the time of the trip I'm remembering, Roberta and I had been married for just over three years. Kate, of course, has known only her. Andrew liked her best from the start: it pleasures me to watch the immediacy and intimacy in their way of being together. When he first sees her, he starts running toward her; then he leaps up into her arms for a hug. With about another six months of growth, he's going to knock her over when he does that. I don't much think she'll mind. I expect they'll just lie there giggling. After a while, he hugs me. When we go outside to smoke (we don't smoke at Mindy's house; she's part of the Anti-Smoking Force, and they are everywhere), Andrew tells Roberta that if she smokes a cigarette, she will die, and he doesn't want her to die. He doesn't say anything about my pipe. Saturday night when they were playing, Andrew asked her if she wouldn't like to stay there forever. ¶Do you reckon that I am jealous of Andrew? I'm not. He gives good testimony to my good taste. ¶Kate doesn't say much. Mostly she smiles beautifully and goes ahead doing what they've just told her not to do. ¶The four of them have a good, sweet, busy life, and they are dear together. ¶And so I was puzzled by myself, as I usually am, when we left on Sunday morning and through the trip back. It's not far—about 150 miles—but there's plenty of time to think. ¶By the time we reached Clyde, the first little town on the way back, I was pretty down and out, wishing I could do and be everything for them, wishing I could always assure that life would be and give all they wanted. ¶By the time we reached Baird, the next town, I had remembered a letter written in 1900 and quoted in John Graves's book *Goodbye to a River.* A woman in Kentucky writes to her sister, who had come with her family to Texas. She remembers that it has been twenty-five years, and concludes her letter: "O dear sister, we are not like to see each other any more." ¶By the time we reached Putnam, the little town that died, I was wondering why I find it so hard to be serious with all four of them, so hard to tell all four how much I love them, so hard to tell them how privileged I feel. ¶We played tapes—the Eagles, Willie Nelson, Beethoven—and drove on, past Cisco and Eastland and Ranger, down Ranger Hill, by Thurber, after a while on by Weatherford, to home. ¶Long before we reached Fort Worth, I'd have been really sad, but I was with Roberta. When we got back, there was still time for me to finish turning a piece of the yard into a new flower bed. She was inside doing chores. After a while, everything was almost all right. ¶I guess I know that, no matter how many times you go to or through or by a place, you don't ever see it again. Still, I ask, as Maggie Anderson's poem puts the question, "Why can't we hold this landscape in our arms?" ¶Many of the places I have seen, I will not see again because they are gone. The shotgun house in Jayton is gone. Did it have two rooms or three, and where did we all sleep—my mother, my father, my brother, and me? The two-room house down the road from Grandpa's farm is gone. What was our furniture like? Did we own much? The house by the Sproule's place in Jayton is gone. Jimmy Mathews's house is gone. The house at 801 Sylvania is gone, and the house at 3015 Bird and the house at 3319 Bellaire Drive North. The railroad trestle below Grandpa's farm house is gone, and the house is gone. The Big Rock Candy Mountain is gone. I remember them. I see them. ¶Perhaps the Christian Hell is, as a friend used to say, only an eternity of regret, and we can't walk through to the other side. Usually, as Stephen Dobyns's poem "North Wind" says, life "feels much too complicated to reach a place of contentment." Steven Bauer's poem "Old Faithful" recalls a visit to the geyser and the unstable ground around. That night, the poem ends,

> In the dark there were no tourists,
> no signs to tell me which
> of all the ground was safe, if any was.

None is altogether safe. Arnold M. Eisen's *Galut* reminds me that "in the beginning, there was exile." ¶Many places that I wanted to see, I will not see. Many places that I have seen, I will not see. Many places I will not see because they are gone. Still, I remember, even if imperfectly. Once, years ago, when I was a young, sometimes impudent, assistant professor, a senior professor was extolling "that incomparable Greek light" to a group of us who had been chatting. Without waiting to think, I said, "Why, hell, Mabel, haven't you ever been in West Texas on a stunning November day, very like this one?"

Not Filed

I have not been able to keep what I've lost and know I've lost.
I have not been able to keep what I've lost but don't know I've lost.
I have not been able to keep what I never knew.
I can remember but not keep what I have gone off and left.
I have not been able to keep what I chose not to see in the first place.
I must keep but cannot remember what I have repressed.

I like to look at fountain pens, and to feel of them,
and to write with them. I cannot fully account for this, but
I enjoy it anyway. Opportunities for looking, therefore feeli
aren't all that common. Drug stores and grocery stores and
other stores that carry school supplies usually have ~~all~~ lots
of pencils, markers, and ballpoint pens, but no fountain pens,
~~unlessxxikix~~ though a few have the inexpensive Sheaffer Cartrid
~~pen~~ Fountain Pen. Office supply stores usually have fountain
mostly quite expensive. Some university book stores keep a
supply of fountain pens, also usually expensive, and, I daress
intended as gifts. Art and hobby supply shops usuall have per
and sets of pens for the uses of those who practice calligrap
The best place for looking, therefore feeling, in my experienc
has been ~~the~~ Gilbertson Clybourns, Inc., Purveyors of Fine Wri
Instruments, formerly of 540 N. Michigan Avenue, inside the
Marriott Hotel in Chicago, now to be located farther up the
street near the Water Tower. For the past ten years, I've gor
every fall with my wife to Chicago, where she attends a meetir
I find it entirely pleasant to be kept. She's busy during the
day, and I'm free to walk about the city. I always go call up
the ~~Purvek~~ Purveyors of Fine Writing Instruments so that I may
visit the fountain pens, look at them, and perhaps feel of one
or two. The shop has the largest selections I have seen, Cros
pens, Sheaffers, Parkers, Waternmans, Mont Blancs, others. Th
are long and short, fat and lean, sleek silver, ~~xinx~~ shiny bla
checkered silver and black, gold, with an occasional bold red

Active Files

I like to look at fountain pens, and to feel of them and to write with them. I cannot fully account for this, but I enjoy it anyway. Opportunities for looking, therefore feeling, aren't all that common. Drug stores and grocery stores and other stores that carry school supplies usually have lots of pencils, markers, and ballpoint pens, but no fountain pens, though a few have the inexpensive Sheaffer Cartridge Fountain Pen. Office supply stores usually have fountain pens, mostly quite expensive. Some university book stores keep a supply of fountain pens, also usually expensive, and, I daresay, intended as gifts. Art and hobby supply shops usually have pens and sets of pens for the use of those who practice calligraphy. The best place for looking, therefore feeling, in my experience has been Gilbertson Clybourns, Inc., Purveyors of Fine Writing Instruments, formerly of 540 N. Michigan Avenue, inside the Marriott Hotel in Chicago, now to be located farther up the street near the Water Tower. For the past ten years, I've gone every fall with my wife to Chicago, where she attends a meeting. I find it entirely pleasant to be kept. She's busy during the day, and I'm free to walk about the city. I always go call upon the Purveyors of Fine Writing Instruments so that I may visit the fountain pens, look at them, and perhaps feel of one or two. The shop has the largest selection I've seen: Cross pens, Sheaffers, Parkers, Watermans, Mont Blancs, others. They are long and short, fit and lean, sleek silver, shiny black, checkered silver and black, gold, with an occasional bold red and several of the really elegant ones in marbled blue or marbled maroon. Some are quite ornate and exotic—I think in particular of Mont Blanc's Agatha Christie Special, upon which a gold coiled snake forms the clip. I haven't bought a pen there. I can't afford them, but I have surely enjoyed looking. ¶In the past few years, however, I have collected a few nice pens. I have several of the big, inexpensive Sheaffer Cartridge Fountain Pens that I keep in the various places where I'm likely to find myself. I own two nice Sheaffer pens, a black one that I bought for myself, a green one that my wife brought to me from a shop in France. I own a handsome Diplomat pen that leaks and a handsome Pelican pen that doesn't. And now, I own the perfect pen. She gave it to me just last week. ¶Fountain pens, as you may be able to tell, are important to me. ¶I hope some small remnant of writing survives me. If it does, it will leave my hands as a manuscript done with a fountain pen or as a typescript done on a manual, not an electric, typewriter. I don't, you see, use the funny new machines. I'm glad that others do. That I don't may be owing to simple, sheer perversity, though I like to think that I have some reasons, however insufficient they may seem to others. ¶I don't know always why for one piece of work I use the typewriter, for another the fountain, or why most often, I start with a fountain pen, and then, when I've written enough to see where I'm going, I shift to the typewriter. At my advanced age, I expect it's largely instinct and impulse deriving from habit and past performance, but so long as I get the work done, I'm willing to trust instinct and impulse. ¶I use the two instruments for reasons that are sometimes personal, silly, and trivial, but my own and probably insufficient for others, though I do think that people ought to pay more attention than they usually seem to, to their own physical and psychological character, to their own tempos and feelings. Not everyone should be cajoled, seduced, taught, or made to use the same instrument. While there may be dark and foolish reasons too well-hidden for me to find for my continuing to use the manual typewriter, some of my reasons are simple, personal, and practical. I like the reverie time my manual typewriter affords. When you stop to correct a foolish mistake on the word processor, you have to think about what you're doing. When you use liquid paper, you don't, and sometimes in that marvelous free moment while it dries, an entire new paragraph takes shape. I can't afford the time it would take to become as proficient and comfortable and as fast with a new machine as I am with my old machine. I am stubborn. I want change to be self-generated (as in my instruments for writing), not brought about because someone thinks it's for my own good. And the manual typewriter accommodates me physically. I hit the keys hard. I like to slam the carriage back. It's wonderfully satisfying when the work goes poorly, wonderfully exhilarating when the work goes well. Each morning when I address my Olympia manual typewriter, I ask it to last as long as I do. The company doesn't make manuals any more, and ribbons are hard to find. My existence depends upon this machine. ¶Still, if I had to choose, I'd choose the fountain pen. ¶Perhaps it's just arthritis. My hands are somewhat afflicted, so that after a couple of hours at the typewriter, I tend to wince and to sob a little. My fountain pen is easy to hold. ¶I'd guess that there's more to it than that would suggest. The first lessons we learn, in whatever area of our lives, are powerful. They influence and direct our lives even when we don't know it, even when we don't want them to, even when we've learned better. After initial lessons in learning to print, initial lessons in penmanship, I learned to write with a fountain pen. I am not able or willing to give that up. Even now, when I think about Samuel Johnson and all the work he managed to get done without our wondrous machines—the great dictionary, the edition of Shakespeare, all the *Rambler* and *Idler* essays, a play, a novel, the *Lives of the Poets,* and all the rest—I feel a little guilty if I even use my manual typewriter and think maybe that if I would slow down and use my pen, work harder, think harder, I might do better. ¶Perhaps our myths, if they can be called myths, are not beautiful, but only powerful. Probably myth isn't the right word. I don't know what the right word is. I'm still trying to find it. I'm looking for a word or phrase that will say what we have kept without knowing we have kept it, that will name the lore we enact without knowing that we do so, that will name those almost inescapable first lessons, that will identify what shapes our eyeballs to see as they do. I know what food is. Frozen food isn't food, though I sometimes eat it. Canned food isn't food, though I sometimes eat it. Food brought in isn't food, though I sometimes eat it. Food is what's prepared from scratch by one's own hand. Writing isn't writing unless it begins with a fountain pen. I know some of the reasons that I believe as I do, but I daresay I don't know all of them. A fiction that I didn't invent directs my thoughts and behavior. ¶When, after generations and centuries of human enterprise with ample opportunity for observation, someone tells the story of Echo and Narcissus, we learn to see in it in an astute descriptive analysis of ourselves, and know that we're always in peril, like Echo, of alienation from ourselves, and, like Narcissus, of excommunication from others. We hear that story, applaud its wisdom, call it a *classical myth,* and call it beautiful. We need our myths, Karsten Harries says, in our attempt to escape the tyranny of physical time and the terror of a world that appears indifferent to our needs and hopes. Myth is born of the human inability to accept that we and all we have created someday will be past, will have vanished without a trace, unremembered and unredeemed. To feel at home in the world, we have to be able to interpret whatever presents itself in such a way that it answers to our needs. ¶Yes. As we read our myths, so shall we interpret. I'm looking, however, for another word to name the stories that direct, predict, control our thoughts, actions, beliefs, stories that we didn't invent, but acquired, usually without knowing that we did so. ¶Roland Barthes calls them *ideologies,* these stories or sermons that, while they may eventually give us interpretations, for now give us instructions. I believe that I understand his intention in this, and I think he is as right as can be in proposing that our lives are ideologically driven. Still, *ideology* doesn't seem to be the right word to me, since I have another definition for ideology of which I cannot rid myself—a conception of ideology as a deliberately created system of belief, thought, or action. But I'm talking about systems that we inherit, acquire, take in by osmosis. Perhaps I'll just call them *sermons,* directions that we receive and follow, usually without knowing that we do so. ¶We are not so much less than the ancients. Some of our sermons are beautiful, too, but seldom lead us through green pastures or by still waters. I am, I believe, author of wonderful fantasies in my mind, capable of extravagant, even flamboyant behavior in private commerce, but some sermon directs my body to be monogamous, directs my attitude to be, sometimes at least, overtly prim and prudish. Last week my beautiful young step-daughter visited us to do her laundry. Before she began, she brought in a load of our laundry from the dryer and folded all of it. Included in the load she brought in was some of my underwear. I was horrified, though silent: she should not even have seen my underwear, let alone folded it. ¶Some of the people who preached my sermons were beautiful, too. Joe Dimaggio was beautiful, and Nevada and Lassiter and Shane and Sydney Carton and the Scarlet Pimpernel and Heathcliff and Hopalong Cassidy and Scorchy Smith and Zorro. They and John Calvin preached sermons so compelling and so strong that they have often controlled my body and most of my mind. ¶The sermons slip into us, make themselves known to us when we are unaware. In Rodney Jones's poem, "A Slide of the Ladies Home Missionary Meeting," the speaker recalls learning the lesson of such a sermon:

> Since I drove up toward a cemetery
> With a girl and we lay down half-naked
> And rose up naked, with the horns blaring
> And the long row of headlights shining
> In our eyes, I've studied to memorize
> The ground rules in the South: (1) God's
> Watching all the time; (2) Every cemetery
> Hides a church.

These sermons are always present and active, forming the first lessons that we learned without knowing that we had learned them. I can't begin to locate or to identify all of them, though I know some of them. ¶I've already mentioned lessons I learned from hymns—they're sermons, too. I obeyed them without thought and failed them without exception. Some sermons, ideologies, myths, however, I can recognize. Sometimes, I guess, sermons are not just our silent system of instructions, but also, with time, grow into myths of interpretive power. I know that somehow, somewhere, I learned that I must be *proper,* though I haven't been. I learned that I must *work* diligently, incessantly, and intensely, though I haven't. I learned that I must be a *superpower,* though I'm not, and I learned that the world ought to be *quiet,* though it isn't. ¶Of the first of these alone, I know the provenance. I took lessons in propriety—and I might as well add the other part, virtue—from my

Mother. Where she found her scriptures on a scraggly farm I don't know. Probably I was misinformed about her parents, my grandparents. Probably she sprang full grown from the mating of John Calvin with Lady Pearl. She was a gentlewoman, proper, virtuous, and strong. She was also tougher than a boot, and she could outwork just about any strong man except, perhaps, my father. He liked to brag about the cotton-picking season when she was sixteen: she was the only one in the county to pick over 500 pounds of cotton in a single day. Her sermons were not extended discourses. They tended to come in short bursts. "Don't be loud in public," she'd say. Or, "Don't call attention to yourself." Or, "That was thoughtless." Or, "Don't be rude to people." Or, "Don't make scenes in public." Or, worst of all, she'd say, "Don't act like poor white trash." I'm still afraid: that's probably just what I turned out to be. Oh, to be sure, I have honored and obeyed her lessons in propriety—in just about all of the trivial ways. In significant matters, I have just about always failed them. I have been unfaithful, improper, and unvirtuous. ¶I don't know exactly how to account for my attitudes about work. A friend, a colleague in the Philosophy Department who doesn't know any better, once said that I was the principal example of the Protestant Work Ethic. Such diagnostic terms are too elevated for my case, and besides, what he said is not entirely true. The other day, a friend remarked that she admired my discipline at work. I appreciated her saying that, but she was wrong. To be disciplined is to have chosen to be disciplined. I have not worked out of a belief in a work ethic. I have worked because I cannot do otherwise without consequence. That doesn't mean that I have always worked, diligently, effectively, incessantly. It does mean that if I don't work, I am wrong for not working. At least until their life became economically a little easier for them, my parents worked without questioning the need for work. They worked because that was their job. The only reward for working is that you're not thrown in jail. I have never worked hard enough. If you don't work, then you're poor white trash and you go to hell. ¶Of the third sermon/myth/ideology that I must be a superpower, I can say little without violating the first, that it must be proper. I learned by diverse means that I should be able to create myself as an authentic individual, perfectly able to handle any chore, need, or crisis, or challenge that presented itself, that I should be a strong cowboy and a perfect knight, that, if at all possible, I should go valiantly to war, that I should be the perfect, imaginative, and untiring lover. In *A Choice of Heroes,* Mark Gerzon writes of what he calls "the changing faces of American manhood." I'm not entirely able to see that we have changed all that much. Much of what I learned—no, not learned, but accepted by osmosis—about who I should be was wrong, but I have not generally been as successful in discarding one false hope for a better. I don't even like the idea of the hero, but I want to be a hero. What seems to happen is that heroic ideals don't change; they accumulate, so that a fellow has to be all of them, or else he's worse than a dismal failure: brave frontiersman, gallant soldier, consistent defender of the underdog, caring and gener- ous breadwinner, loving and caring husband, devoted father, complete expert in all things, lord of all things. ¶God knows what else osmosed, and I was not alone. In Sunday school, for example, Mackenzie Canter learned "that the reason the North won was because Lee, being a Chris- tian, and, in particular, an Episcopalian, wouldn't fight dirty like Sher- man and Sheridan. Lee and Jesus even looked alike, with big, haunting dark eyes that called you to repent, enlist, or both." I yearned, too, to be, as Canter says of some Scotch-Irish Democrats, "ornery by nature and contrarian by philosophy." ¶Knowing the prejudices, errors, mis- conceptions, and sins of this myth with its variants does not mean that we repudiate it, however much we might like to. As James V. Catano says, "The healthy individual does not readily form him or herself, nor do we suddenly discover ourselves as free-standing individuals." I know that I have not made myself, and that there is no myself, perhaps, but a gathering of mythical/ideological symptoms and cultural usages. And myth, Catano acknowledges, appeals to our needs and fears:

> In the case of the myth of the self-made man, these basic needs and fears can be stated in terms of two psychological appeals and their oppositions. The appeals focus on 1) a desire for per- sonal growth and 2) a need to form an acceptable, in this case masculine, identity. Each appeal is countered by an oppos-

go into combat for the tribe, we will not se

and it will not be a failure. If, upon ente

congress, a woman is moved or unmoved, passi

there are no inevitable outward signs. If a

his two chief functions, to enter combat for

for the woman, his failure is immediately an

If, upon entering into sexual congress, a ma

erection, someone is bound to notice, and hi

plain to see.

Some myths, I mean to say, stay with us

mystic runes inside xxxxxxxx that tell xxx f
                                  the

whether John Wayne is a xxxxxxx threat to so

Adam, Garry Wills remarks:

He is both. He is the former because he

He reflects our society back upon itsel

source of his appeal, and of his danger

terrifying image, full of the unresolve

our ideal xxxxxxx country. We may have

left; but neither do we have a cult cit

center to our society. Our meaning lie

or so we seem to think--in the independe

ing force: 1) the desire for self-growth must address the power of institutional determination; 2) the pursuit of masculinity must face the possibility of failure—in the myth's terms, emasculation or feminization.

To this and to other exhortations against the myth of machismo, I can only say yes, adding this condition, that failure is not just possible, it is inevitable. But knowing the prejudices, errors, misconceptions, and sins of this myth with its variants does not mean that we expunge it easily, if at all. For a while yet, and perhaps for a long time, the superpower myth will continue to enact itself, and men will always fail. ¶The myth is powerful and may even be beautiful, in a wry sort of way. Certainly it is deeply rooted in nearly half of us. I'm inclined, indeed, to think that we still have not thought through all the implications of the myth. To those of us who really like them, women are superior. They are complete and sufficient. They do not fail, or, if they do, we do not know it, even if we like to imagine that their physical strength is somewhat less than ours. Quite aside from the two signal powers that only women have—they can get pregnant, and they can breastfeed their young—women have a third great power. If they fail, their failure doesn't show, we don't see it, and so they must be complete and unfailing. If they choose not to go into combat for the tribe, we will not see that as failure, and it will not be a failure. If, upon entering into sexual congress, a woman is moved or unmoved, passionate or dispassionate, there are no inevitable outward signs. If a man fails one of his two chief functions, to enter combat for the tribe, specifically for the woman, his failure is immediately and publicly noticeable. If, upon entering into sexual congress, a man does not have an erection, someone is bound to notice, and his failure will be plain to see. ¶Some myths, I mean to say, stay with us, with me, like the mystic runes inside that tell the future. Asking whether John Wayne is a threat to society or the American Adam, Garry Wills remarks:

He is both. He is the former because he is the latter. He reflects our society back upon itself, which is the source of his appeal, and of his danger. It is a mixed and terrifying image, full of the unresolved contradictions in our ideal country. We have no literal frontier left; but neither do we have a cult city, a temple, a holy center to our society. Our meaning lies still in motion, or so we seem to think—in the independent individual, the need for space as an arena for freedom. Do we really believe that we have escaped the myth of the frontier, the mystique of the gun, the resistance to institutions?

And so, even when I'm trying to be sensible, there's a corner in my mind in which I am sorry that I didn't, after all, turn out to be a brave cowboy or a gallant knight. And, in that small, dark corner of my mind, I should have gone to war. Not going, I have failed. I don't believe that I measure myself against heroes, except for Joe Dimaggio. But I have found myself wanting when I measure myself against ordinary men at Verdun, at Gettysburg, Chancellorsville, Antietam, at Iwo Jima, at the Anzio Beach, at Rorke's Drift, in the Ardennes. No, I doubt that's true. Oftener than not, I expect I have measured myself and found myself wanting against romanticized, fictionalized, cinematized mythologies. ¶But not all compulsions of the superpower myth are toward the grand, however mistaken. Some are simply dumb. I have this legacy, perhaps from all or most males, perhaps chiefly from those tribes that came down and out westering to splendor, death, misunderstanding, disaster, woe. They made a long hard run, came west to prowess, rule, came west to death, in those white centuries, and now, perhaps, their course is done—all come to this, all come to me. ¶An aging, blue-eyed lover, I have pleased and pleasured her, I think, in diverse ways, and have found all ways exceedingly good. She calls to me, searches, shudders, gives some witness, too, that she has found all good as well. And yet I still believe that's not enough. I still believe that I must fire tracers, rockets, bombs—again, again, again, again, again—or else I'm not real, and have not received just testimony to her beauty and love. It's all come to this. How shall I, an aging, blue-eyed lover, turn against the lessons it took centuries to learn, that gave the only character I knew? ¶Perhaps I got them wrong, those lessons. Perhaps I misremembered what was never true. ¶How many myths, ideologies, sermons? Who knows? Because they are myths, ideologies, sermons, they are difficult to locate. ¶I should mention one other, though I may have invented it all by myself. I thought the world was supposed to be quiet. What that means, I guess, is that I want the world to be quiet. I need the world to be quiet. It is very loud in here; I don't need noise out there. Perhaps this is only because I grew up, part of the way, in a small rural community, and I could sometimes spend days alone. Perhaps I want quiet because, as Mackenzie Canter puts it, I want to believe that "my daily routines were proof against death, that death dare not disturb my rituals of ordinariness." ¶I hope that elsewhere others, mostly younger, have already learned new myths. Almost any sermon would be better than those I've heard: some new path to follow, some imperative to hear, that would let us outrun our own insignificance. But for me, the old myths, ideologies, sermons persist, even when I don't want them to, perhaps especially when I don't want them to persist. They are in my scrapbook. I did not choose to put them there. And so I am left as the speaker is in Robert Fink's poem, "The Hot Corner":

The third baseman
has a wife and kids,
always a baby needing shoes,
and he's in a crapshoot
with the dice loaded
against him—the one-hopper
to his groin,
the screaming liner to his skull,
the shot pulled down the line
to clip the bag with him extended
as far as heroically possible
and it ain't enough.

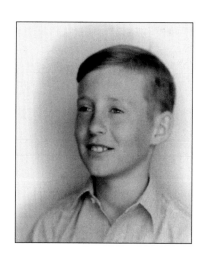

I Am Not Here

What I've lost and know that I've lost is not here. What I've lost and don't know that I've lost is not here. What I never knew is not here, and what I chose not to see. What I've gone off and left is not here, and what I've repressed. What I've sealed away and will not tell is not here. And I'm not here. ¶I spent a good part of my professional life wanting to believe and to show that it is possible to learn each other, to understand a speaker's character or a writer's character if we paid close enough attention to the text the speaker or writer produced. I believed that I was following Aristotle's suggestion regarding the character or *ethos* of a speaker, probably the most important means of connection and of persuasion between a hearer or reader and a speaker or writer. I published academic papers testifying that I had learned the character of various speakers and writers—Abraham Lincoln, Samuel Johnson, Shane, the prophet Amos, others. ¶I was partly right. ¶I think I did a pretty good job in describing the characters *in the texts that I read.* But of course Abraham Lincoln was somebody apart from his speeches and Samuel Johnson was somebody apart from his *Rambler* essays, and Amos was somebody I couldn't find at all, and even the fictional Shane was somebody outside the story Shaeffer tells. What I found and wrote about, I think, does help to account for the appeal of these speakers, but the texts I studied don't contain their characters any more than my scant text contains the self that I imagine that I am or want to be. ¶And besides, after all these years, I have come to think that my project was suspicious from the outset. ¶My interest in the project began in the late 1960s, when conflict, commotion, confrontation, and (at least impending) evil seemed to be everywhere. I think I wanted to believe that our wars with each other could be avoided or settled if we could, out of our separate worlds and from our separate rhetorics, learn to hear each other and to understand. I think I wanted to believe that we could notice each other, acknowledge each other, genuinely know each other. I still believe that, as of course most of us do, and as I wrote those academic papers, I wanted to believe that I was studying speakers and writers who had by honest and open means found audiences and that I was trying to learn what had enabled audiences to listen. I think I was generally right in what I wrote, as far as that went. ¶But I didn't go far enough. ¶Gradually, over the years, I began to see that I hadn't sufficiently examined my own motives. To be sure, I did want to learn how speakers and writers had come to be known and to be heard by audiences, and I still do. Ever so slowly, however, I came to see that I didn't first of all want to notice, to acknowledge, to know other speakers and writers—I had come to this study, I finally had to recognize, because I wanted to learn how to get others to notice, to acknowledge, and to know me. I didn't want to die of my own insignificance. ¶And I didn't go far enough in another respect. I had already begun to learn, of course, that the author was not in his or her text and that readers and hearers kidnapped the text to make of it what they might. But I didn't learn that lesson in a personal, intimate, and emotional way until a short time ago, when I was reading some reviews of a couple of my books that were published recently. They were, in general, well-received, though seldom read. One review sticks in my mind. The reviewer was nice and said some wonderfully pleasant things about the book he was reviewing. I was tickled, and I danced a little jig, and I thought I would just make a run for fame and fortune. Toward the end of his account, the reviewer fell to talking about what he called my *voice,* and allowed as how he thought he had come to know me through the book. Perhaps he had. Perhaps what he read was all there is to me. ¶I didn't think so at the time. I caught myself backing away from the review. I heard myself saying, "Wait just a damn minute. You don't know me. There's more to me than what you've found." There I was, denying what I had earlier written, that we could learn the character of a speaker or writer in what he or she had said or written. The reviewer had not learned me, I thought, and of course he had. I am not there, and of course I am. It's hard not to find each other, hard not to be noticed, acknowledged, known, hard not to find oneself, in the past tense or any other. ¶In his poem, "Two Houses Away," David Keller writes of his neighbor:

> My neighbor is trying to change shape,
> to die. Each day he's thinner, he eats less,
> trying to slip out of the body, the boy
> he remembers over seventy years ago.

We look for selves, find them, lose them, discover that they've changed while we weren't looking. I have two snapshots of myself taken when I was a boy. The first shows a skinny, goofy-looking kid. He wears baggy slacks, a short-sleeved knit shirt, and a baseball cap, shoved to the back of his head. He has a baseball glove on his left hand. He is perhaps thirteen. He is a stranger to me. A ball is in the glove. I know it is myself because I know it is myself. ¶The second snapshot was made earlier. The boy is in the second grade, probably eight years old. He stands in the lower center of the picture, on a rock at the bottom of a canyon. The wall of canyon slants upward maybe twenty feet above his head. A single mesquite stands on top, to the boy's right. The boy's hair is blond, and seems almost white on his sunlit side. He is wearing his church-going clothes—trousers, cuffed, with a trace of a crease in the legs, a shirt, probably white, and, of all things, a tie. It must be Sunday, else he'd not be wearing such things. It is probably 1937, perhaps early 1938. He is a stranger to me. I know it is myself because I know it is myself. ¶The possibilities of representation, we have learned only in our century, are closely limited. We can't render, recreate, or represent the thing, the place, the other, as it was, though we can render, recreate, and represent what we believe we have perceived, in whatever our chosen medium allows. ¶Certainly we haven't always represented ourselves well, though some of our representations in arts and letters are the best thing about us. ¶Some men, I'm pretty sure, have hidden away some of their features and attitudes, leaving others, especially women, to see only what makes men appear to be dominators, owners, brutes, asses, apes, knaves, fools, or all of the above. Perhaps most of us can do little about it if we turn out to be asses or fools, but if we had been able to present ourselves more honestly and directly, we might have been spared being thought dominators, brutes, apes, or knaves. If, for example, we are taken to be dominators, wanting "to take care of the little woman," that may happen not because we think women are inferior creatures, but because we believe that they are superior, all of them, and we want to serve them, to be their knights. Men have not, however, done a particularly successful job of representing themselves in that way. And if, for example, we are taken to be owners (at least would-be owners), we may have encouraged that interpretation by our failures in self-representation. When we paint, carve, or photograph nude women, it has frequently been said of us that when we do so, and when we view these nudes, we have done so in possession, the women having been pictured or carved for the delight of the unpictured and uncarved but always present male viewer. I expect that is true. I also expect that it is not true enough. Over the centuries, I think, some of us have made such nude images and some of us have looked at them not because we sought to own the women, but because we wanted to pay tribute to them. Women are life, and women are the most beautiful features of creation. We wanted to pay tribute, and it was never enough: too often our tributes seemed to be efforts to possess. I should add that, oftener than not, we did turn out to be dominators, owners, brutes, asses, apes, knaves, fools, and all of the above. ¶Whichever I turn out to be, I am not here. I began to fade when I was born, I think, never emerging into life, never entirely representing myself into life, or being represented, fading at last to nothing. Even now, as I bang on my typewriter, I wonder if this is the last day. My manual typewriter is old, and I am older. Arthritis makes knobs out of my knuckles. My circulation is poor. My finger tips are mostly numb. My hands are cold. They hurt up to my shoulder. Besides, they don't make ribbons any more for my machine. We leave pale signs, where I had hoped for bolder. Or maybe I died some while ago. Maybe this is the afterlife. Perhaps I am outside looking in, not showing to all those others, who seem in sepia to me, not appearing on their maps. They doubt I'm here or know I'm not. No minicam will catch me, and no Kodak will hold me as I am, for I am not and was not. Or maybe I am inside looking out, put away to be responsible alone for what I've done, my fingers curled around the bars of my cell, the cell that keeps them safe out there. Whichever, I'm apart, or not here, I think, though I'm not sure. Perhaps I just can't understand whatever evidence there is to make some sense or to be assured. I'm not here, not even to myself. ¶ But it was effrontery and error to expect to be here. I should have known about the effrontery of it. That time when I was eight and I asked my mother what color my hair was and she told me it was "kind of a turd-muckledy-dun," that was her way of telling me not to think very much or very often of myself. I should have listened and known. Perhaps she also knew about the error of expecting to be a self, present in the world. ¶ If there is anywhere in the neighborhood a self that is not merely selfish, it is hard to find. Autobiography, as Heller and Wellbery put it, is only "the artificial construction of an integrated self against the background of the fragmented history of any actual life…." In "To Write: An Intransitive Verb?" Roland Barthes remarks that "the *I* of the one who writes *I* is not the same as the *I* which is read by *thou.*" Writing about "peculiar problems for a poet in some of the conditions in Western Europe and America since the Second World War," Barbara Everett remarks that

> … there will be little point in counting on any belief, in practice, in the truth or even the existence of the individual's interior self. The very word "imagination," once used to gesture toward an inner life beyond the surface, is as dated and unusable as the concept itself.

And yet I am here. In the Preface to *Formations of Fantasy,* Victor Burgin, James Donald, and Cora Kaplan remark that "psychoanalysis recognises no state of totally unambiguous and self-possessed lucidity in which an external world may be seen for, and known as, simply what it is." There is no possible "end to ideologies." No matter how I have been constructed by my parents, my training, my culture, I am sometimes quite alone. No matter how much the language writes me, I am sometimes quite alone. No one lives in precisely the history I live in. No one

save me looks out through my eyes. I am here, though unreliable. ¶If I did know the truth about something, I might not be able to say it usefully to another. Sometimes I am only Echo, unable to say anything except in the public language that everyone uses, therefore alienated from myself. Sometimes I am only Narcissus, unable to say anything except in my private language, therefore excommunicated from others. And more: I am always the one who knows and the one who doesn't know. I am here, fuzzy around the edges, and unreliable. ¶I may not, then, be able to make a good or even accurate representation of what I think I may know, including myself, but in some circumstances, I can make the only representation of what I think I may know. If I don't remember and tell about my grandfather and grandmother or the porch of their farm house, about my other grandmother's quilts, about my mother and "turd-muckledy-dun," about my father and the doughnuts, about my brother and his football team, about Putoff Canyon, then who will? I am responsible for them and for what I remember. ¶I cannot be present as in an integrated self with inerrant memory. I am a gathering of sometimes misremembered small particulars, loosely stitched together so that great holes are plain between them. I watch students on the campus and often see them marking "main points" in their textbooks, in pale yellow or pale blue or pale red. I think that is appropriate: "main points" are pale, though they may be interesting and mildly revelatory. But they are unsituated; they hold no life. We have to tell life as best we can in its particulars if we are to tell history and philosophy. ¶I am glad to be able to remember that I was sad during our trip to Washington in 1993, and to be able to remember that the sadness was situated. We arrived on Saturday, October 30, late in the afternoon, and did little except have a pleasant seafood dinner with a friend. On Sunday, October, 31, we had lunch with her cousins and whiled away the afternoon at the Smithsonian. We had dinner at a restaurant called Thai Taste near the hotel and dropped in at Murphy's Irish Bar to listen to the music. The young man sang a nice mix of Irish music and his own satirical songs, one of which had this refrain: "I'll sing anything, even 'God save the Queen,' / But I just won't sing Bob Dylan." On Monday, November 1, we lazed away the morning, had lunch nearby, at Taste of India, then walked and looked all afternoon in Georgetown, returning to have dinner near the hotel, at Petitto's. My wife would be busy for the next two days at her meeting, and I would walk. On Tuesday, November 2, I walked as far as I could, though I stayed within the city in the northwest quadrant. I looked around in Bick's Books on 18th Street Northwest and in Kramer's Books on Connecticut Avenue. I was able to make it back to Murphy's Irish Bar for a drink before I met her. On Wednesday, November 2, I walked again. I stopped in for a Bloody Mary at Mr. Eagan's Bar, just below the Dupont Circle. I browsed in Chapters Bookstore on K Street Northwest and in Olsson's Books on 19th Street Northwest. I stopped twice at Graybeards, a pipe and tobacco shop just below the Dupont Circle, the second time to buy the pipe I had lusted after on the first visit. Once again I made it by Murphy's Irish Bar for a drink. ¶All the while, I wondered about my older daughter. Wherever I walked those days, she was somewhere within a couple of miles of where I was, but I didn't see her. I paused before the office where she once worked, at 1834 Connecticut Avenue Northwest. I paused halfway across the Taft Bridge to look at the autumn colors below and to look all around, wondering where she was, wondering, too, what would happen if she chanced to look out a window and see me walking along below. Would she want to catch up with me and visit? Would she turn away again? I guess I knew the answers. On Thursday, November 4, we came home. ¶The only evidence I have of others, usually, is in the shape or style of what they do and say and in the occasion and audience to which they act and think. Usually, I have little, if any, of their history. Of myself, I have some historical evidence, but it is incomplete. I can't tell myself to myself. I can't tell myself to you. You can't tell me yourself. We won't altogether know each other. When I speak or write, I have already dropped off much of the structure, therefore the meaning of what I say or write, and I have already dropped off much of the history of whatever I may say or write. ¶Nothing, including myself, is fixed and stable and entirely real. We decide what is real; we live a rhetorical process. We live arguments, where versions of reality, whether within ourselves or between ourselves and others, come into contest, where decisions about reality encounter. Identity is a continuing rhetorical enactment, a continuing investigation of the revealing though finally irrecoverable archive and of the structural and stylistic maneuvers by which we decide what is real. Fuzzy around the edges and unreliable, we are here, and each of us is unique, as David Lowenthal puts it: "Experience is not only unique; more significantly, it is also self-centered; I am a part of your milieu, but not of my own, and never see myself as the world does." We always leave ourselves behind, but I want you to know where I like to think I was.

The Buried Tin

I have lost some things that I know I've lost. I have lost much that I don't know I've lost. I have lost all that I never knew. I have lost what I went off and left. I have lost what I chose not to see. I have lost what I have repressed. But I have sometimes gone hunting. ¶I started to school in Jayton, Texas, in the fall of 1936. On my birthday that fall, I was seven years old. I know that much. Sometime in the middle of that school year—perhaps it was during the Christmas holiday, or perhaps it was early in the spring term—the cotton oil mill where my father worked closed down for lack of any more cotton crop, and my family moved to a small house in the country about twenty miles to the north of Jayton, where my father worked temporarily for the Highway Department. For the rest of that school year, my brother and I would ride a school bus into Spur, he to the junior high school, I to the elementary school. ¶The house to which we moved was some two or three miles from my grandparents' small farm. I've said that the house was small. That's not exactly accurate. It was tiny. There were two rooms and on the front a small porch. It's not that my recollection of the place is wonderfully correct. It isn't. I have, however, been able to verify some small memories. The house long ago mostly collapsed upon itself, but the ruin is still there, at the corner of a field of mesquites. I have been to see the ruin more than once, and I have been able to step inside a little way, enough to see its original configuration. I can't remember how and where, in that cramped space, my parents, my brother, and I slept and ate. ¶A short way behind the house there was a small shed and, farther away, an outhouse. Little sign is left of the outhouse, and the shed has also partly collapsed. It was originally a three-sided structure, open to the west. I remember the shed, I expect, because I sometimes ran in there to pee when it was dark and I didn't want to go all the way to the outhouse. ¶Sometime probably just after that spring term was over, my father got word that the oil mill was once again taking on the men it had let go, and we moved back to Jayton. Before we moved, something happened that has remained a mystery to me since. ¶Among my few possessions was a small tin lidded box, probably about two and a half by three and a half inches and probably less than an inch deep. A day or so before we left the little house, or maybe even the day we left, I put some small treasures in the box. I think perhaps that included a marble, and a small scrap of paper on which I had written the name (Virginia something) of a pretty little blonde girl in my room at school, and there may have been one or two other tiny items. Then I buried the tin, just inside the open west front of the little shed. It was twenty-seven years before I saw the little house again, and then we only drove by. The house had by that time fallen in upon itself. ¶I have never forgotten burying the tin. As years passed, it came to my mind often, and I wondered why I had buried it and what might have been in it. Another twenty-nine years passed before I decided to go dig it up. By that time, I was sixty-three, though I don't know how that could have happened. ¶In early summer, 1993, we set out on a little trip to West Texas. I was intent upon driving enough in what I thought of as my territory to learn what its borders were. My wife, I believe, was intent upon humoring me. I also intended to try to find and dig up the tin, but I had not told her. I didn't know whether or not the project would work out, and if it did, I wanted to surprise her. I had earlier equipped myself with a new folding GI shovel. ¶We drove far enough in various directions to learn that the borders of my territory were pretty close, scarcely extending beyond Stonewall County, Kent County, and Dickens County. Outside that little region in any direction, I realized right away that I was in strange land. We didn't find the little tin. Didn't even come close. ¶We had driven on highways, farm-to-market roads, and dirt roads, and I had come to doubt seriously the wisdom of the undertaking. Earlier, I had been ill, and I had just finished a year of chemotherapy. I was not strong. Our route along back roads and dirt roads, I came to think, was at best foolish, at worst perilous. If we came to trouble, I thought, I'd not be able to get us out. ¶We drove to the north on the two-lane highway that went past my grandfather's farm and came to the dirt road that was, as far as I knew, the only route into the fallen house and the buried tin. We had not gone onto the dirt road more than 200 yards when, surely enough, we drove into trouble. The road itself was packed hard, but a little way down the narrow lane, sand had washed in recent rains down from the higher field above. I guess I was intent on the little tin; at any rate, I didn't pay enough attention: I drove us up to the axle in the sand, and we were stuck. ¶I got out my new shovel. That entailed telling her about my secret plan to find the little tin. We took turns with the shovel, trying to go dig ourselves out. Didn't work. ¶As it turned out, our circumstance wasn't dire. I walked back to the highway, and before long a kind man in a pick-up stopped and used a chain to pull us out. By that time, she and I already knew, without talking about the matter, that we weren't going any farther on that road. We didn't go on to the fallen house. We didn't dig up the little tin. Perhaps it's still there. ¶I have wondered for years, and I wonder now, why I buried that tin with the trinkets it held in the first place. Was I trying to mark a place where I had been? What kind of archive did I imagine I was creating? I was just seven years old. What was I thinking? Was there already some kind of longing for a saved identity? ¶Sometime, when the weather is right, we will go back and hunt for the treasure. Next time, we will rent a metal detector, and we will watch for deep sand. My wife collects little tins.

A Scrapbook of What's Missing

Sometimes, no matter how rich the dig, an archaeologist cannot find sufficient shards to piece together a particular jar. Sometimes, no matter how copious and momentous (and even accurate, which they won't be) our recollections, we cannot fully reconstruct what happened at a particular time and place, or who we were when we were there. I haven't found the buried tin. If I do find it on the next trip, or on the trip after that, it may not be the tin I wanted to find. ¶And if I do find it, I still won't know exactly why I wanted, perhaps needed, to bury it in the first place. All I can do is look back through the screens of sixty-one years and guess. When I do, I think that I had already, at age seven, learned that I was insignificant. I buried the tin, I think now, because I wanted some marker for myself, some archive that told I was here, even if it was a secret. ¶If that is true—and I think it is—then I have more questions without answers. When, where, why, how had I already learned, at seven, that I was insignificant? Who taught me? If I had already learned that I was insignificant, what were the lessons I learned before that? Oftener than not, I'd guess our first lessons are taught to us quietly and repetitively and inauspiciously, though their reverberations clang loudly all our lives. ¶How do some of us seem to live life without noticing life? How did we learn that? How do some of us live life loving life? How did we learn that? How do some of us live life despairing of it? How did we learn that? How do some of us manage to live life both loving it and despairing of it? Who taught us that? ¶I take great pleasure in sitting quietly in the morning, reading the paper and drinking coffee. I want to do that for as long as possible. I enjoy my little routines and want to keep on following them. I want to read as many more books as possible. I want to smoke my pipe again and again and again. I want to go and look closely at West Texas as many times as I can. I want to lie in my beloved's arms for as long as I can, to hear her words, to keep images of her in my head. I love these things and in them love life. ¶But I have little hope of it. I have already just about disappeared. Such small archives as I might have left have mostly blown away in a cold hard wind come down from the northwest, or they remain buried in a small tin. I love the things that I have just mentioned, and will hold them as tightly as I can, but what I expect is to become a burdensome, incapacitated, drooling old man, and then to die. ¶Someone once said some place that the goal of therapy is to free us *from* anxiety and guilt and to free us *for* appropriate joy. That sounds nice and altogether appropriate, though I'm not sure that you can have the one without the other. Still, sometimes I wonder whether or not anxiety and guilt are the first causes of joylessness. How do we explain the sadness of those who love life but despair of it? Does sadness come upon us before anxiety and guilt? And does knowledge of our own insignificance come before sadness? Do we suffer anxiety and guilt and fall into sadness *because* we have learned our insignificance? I am unable to continue: the words—*anxiety, guilt, sadness, insignificance*—twist and turn and leak into each other. Mostly, I guess, we live in between. ¶But, for as long as I can remember, I have wanted to mark the days, to take notice of the days, to hold them, to celebrate them. I have not done so. I have not been able to do so. To do so would have required that I have two lives and a scrapbook for every day. Even then, each scrapbook would be incomplete. ¶I'd probably have done better to make a scrapbook, or even a list, of what's missing. ¶I have not begun to say all that's missing. I have lost much that I know I've lost. I have lost much that I don't know I've lost. I have lost much that I never knew. I have lost what I went off and left. I have lost what I chose not to see. I have lost whatever I have repressed. ¶I have lost more than I could ever list, and that is not all. I have lost what I have found to be unsayable. That does not mean that I don't know how to say some things, though there are many things that I don't know how to say. I am referring to all I have lost because *I will not tell it.* ¶I don't believe that I am unique in this regard. Surely I am not alone with my secrets, sins, and embarrassments. Everyone, I think, and every tribe and every culture has stories that are put away. We keep some matters private, sometimes choosing not even to tell them plainly to ourselves. Sometimes we can't bear to do so. I do not refer to such matters as we may have put away in our subconscious or unconscious places, but to those thoughts, actions, and events that we know perfectly well but have sealed away from public view, that we know perfectly well but usually will not allow ourselves even a private review. In addition to whatever else we may be, we are mostly scoundrels in private places. Americans know what we did at Hiroshima, but we don't particularly like to face it privately. Americans know what we did to the natives of their continent, but we don't particularly like to scrutinize it in the private places of our mind. Solitary souls have their moments of fear, shame, and weakness that they will not recount, not even in the private autobiography that they are always telling themselves. Some matters will not be put in a scrapbook for others to see or for us to remember. ¶ In what is lost and in what will not be said there are potentially strong and profoundly revealing evidences of ourselves. We can't tell our story without the lost and the unsayable. We have to tell our story. That is who we are, the only particularization of our meaning. We cannot tell our stories. What is lost is lost; we can search and find some of it, but not all. In shame, embarrassment, fear of being found totally self-centered and entirely insignificant, we will not say the unsayable.

The Scrapbook That Holds the Truth at the End of the World

Sigmund Freud was my father. ¶He was in this country, though probably not in the right season to sire me. ¶Still, you never know. He was crafty and sometimes wise, and might have done the job. ¶On Mondays and Thursdays, I doubt it. He and my mother wouldn't have moved in the same circles or gone to the same dances. She probably wouldn't have consented. He probably wasn't up to rape. Besides, he smoked cigars and might have been her father, too, and she was chaste, whether by principle or by poverty of choice. I'm no longer sure. ¶I got the genes remembered almost right, though. I inherited the maladies he created as best I could, though I'd guess that I failed in some notable dark particulars. ¶But maybe the little girl from West Texas wasn't my mother. Perhaps I wasn't born. I had to be invented so that the whole entire total twentieth century could enact its foolishness, find a place for its trivialities and, sometimes, sins. ¶If that is so, that makes necessity my mother. ¶I am, at any rate, a child of the century, on a fifty-year binge. Someone may wait a moment here to wonder why I call myself a child, why I say it's fifty years, why I call it a binge. Well, I call myself a child because I'm still waiting to grow up. I say it's fifty years because that's my age, less some tidy years for the indecision we call innocence, and maybe just because fifty seemed enough. I say it's a binge because it is.

Snapshot 1: at the defense of her dissertation, the candidate passes, but the professor fails. The candidate before us is lovely. I have admired her mind and told her bits and pieces, have enjoyed her soul, sentences, legs. She took her B.A. here, her M.A. there, will teach yonder, comes now to present her breasts and dissertation. She is lovely. She owns the world. I pay rent. She knows things. I guess. Tell me, Miss X, what dear secrets would I learn between your legs? Do others know the mystery of earth while I clearly don't? Who exists while I am ghostly, ludicrous in the halls? I could hold her and the committee at bay, could say, "You've done splendid work, Miss X. Before you get away, please take off your clothes. I must see your good shoulders, straight back, and the curve down and out of your splendid hips. Your belly, I do not doubt, is magic. Please Miss X, your thighs would let me know that I exist."

Snapshot 2: in an unnamed bar near campus, regarding certain female and male blondes who are manufactured in a secret place for the purpose of occupying university campuses. The young women are tanned, handsome, often beautiful. They give evidence of long tan legs even when they are short. They look at each other over lunch with earnest regard and high attention but do not see each other, or me. Their look is elsewhere, after all. If you get their attention, they may not run over you with their cars, which are new. If you get their attention, they may marry you, but not see you. If you get their attention, they may become active alumnae. The young men are undressing the young women with their eyes, smiling at something just behind their heads, thinking hot thoughts and cold beer.

Hear, oh hear the night bird call—
Soon, oh soon the dark must fall.

Snapshot 3: late afternoon, with a hotdog and the house's best cheap white wine. Just as a young woman passes by the crowded table nearby, where they're working a fourth pitcher of beer, a young man seated there says, "Shit." I expect him to leap up and to apologize to her, but he seems not to notice. I expect her to faint, or turn and slap the coarse offender, but she seems not to notice. I am astonished: what has the world come to, I wonder, where have sensibilities gone, and old values? Then I go about my life, violating creation every day, smearing metaphors of shit across the lawns, divans, white tablecloths of the civilized world, hoping they don't notice me, or, if they notice me, hoping they won't hold me to accounts.

Hear, oh hear the night bird call—
Soon, oh soon the dark must fall.

Snapshot 4: in the exercise room. They say I'm looking fit. I have lost weight and my belly's firm. My legs still work. My teeth are okay. My mind is all right—a little rot beneath, a few dead twigs above. My pulse is slow, blood pressure nice, color adequate, cholesterol low. I exercise a lot, you see. I run to keep from thinking, work so I won't feel. I practice aerobic dodging. Self One spars with Self Three, Self Five with Self Two. I do isometric strains, setting a yell against a shout so that I won't scream.

Hear, oh hear the night bird call—
Soon, oh soon the dark must fall.

Snapshot 5: at prayer. I've tried for stroke and heart attack, but my body won't cooperate. I doubt I'll sag or burst or blush toward God. I thought I'd catch cancer, rot toward death, die soon if I did it right, but when I did, they cut on me for three or four hours, poisoned me for a year, and pronounced me well. I've had no luck: I prayed, but caught the wrong cancer.

Hear, oh hear the night bird call—
Soon, oh soon the dark must fall.

I tell what I can myself of myself, for myself, believing that it is not just about myself, or wanting to believe. The speaker in Pat Barker's *The Ghost Road* records this in his journal: ¶Posted to the 2nd Manchesters. We leave tomorrow. ¶It's evening now, and everybody's scribbling away, telling people the news, or as much of the news as we're allowed to tell them. I look up and down the dormitory and there's hardly a sound except for pages being turned, and here and there a pen scratching. It's like this every evening. And not just letters either. Diaries. Poems. At least two would-be poets in this hut alone. ¶Why? you have to ask yourself. I think it's a way of claiming immunity. First-person narrators can't die, so as long as we keep telling the story of our own lives we're safe. Ha bloody fucking Ha. ¶He's right, of course, and, as he acknowledges at the end, he's also not right. We die, leaving behind a few scraps that someone may recognize, perhaps, for a generation. Still, I like my scraps and wish I had more. Sometimes I wish I had kept, could keep everything, or almost.

Snapshots 6–11: drunk. Various poses, various moments, some quite recent. Not displayed, not kept, but vivid enough to remember. ¶Sometimes, we can even catch and keep moments of elation long enough to show them to another. Moments of public exhilaration and elation don't last long once the parade is over, but they can sometimes be kept and shown in history books. Moments of private exhilaration and elation last little longer, but some say they are too personal to show, even if we could keep them. Perhaps so. Sometimes I regret that. Moments of regret seem to come oftener.

Snapshot 12: in regret. This is blurred, but I am remembering wishing that I had paid close attention to everyone, to every thing, to every place, all the time.

Snapshot 13: in regret. I wish I could remember how the furniture was arranged in the house at 1033 Cleckler Street, where my family lived when I was in high school. Also blurred.

Snapshot 14: in regret. We had little money. I wish we had had a big station wagon or a van so that our children could have traveled in more comfort when they were small. Also blurred, out of focus. ¶Too many pictures. Too many pictures. Once you start taking pictures of regret with your Brownie box camera, there's no leaving off for some of us. ¶Puzzlement, I think, is my commonest circumstance. Despite my own wishes that I had kept everything, I'm still puzzled why I would want to do so. Snapshots of pain call back pain. Snapshots of exhilaration also call back pain. Probably I should dwindle into a quiet, useless old man with no expectations. I have enjoyed moments of rare happiness.

I have enjoyed moments of wonderful impatience, curiosity, and long-ing. I have enjoyed dear moments of solitude and loneliness. I have no snapshots of these moments nor any that might show who I am.

Journal clipping, September 25, 1997. My birthday. Until this very day, I've had childish notions that one day I'd be a self, or someone else, maybe even visible, that one day everything will be all right. Every-thing will not be all right. No happy ending waits. If I try to be honest, how much do I nevertheless hide? How much do I fictionalize? Is it possible to be honest? Often, I cancel my brain and try not to think. Sometimes I can do that successfully—when I go to the library for fun, when I read the morning paper and work the crossword puzzle. When I am able to work intensely, I can usually leave off thinking, at least about myself. And drinking helps. I often think about lonesome places and want to be there. Each fall, I keep track of the football scores from the smallest towns in West Texas, where the high schools can only field six-man teams. If I were in one of those lonesome places, no one would know where I am. No one could find me to hold me accountable.

Journal clipping, September 29, 1997. There isn't any truth down there, old buddy. If there is, I haven't come close, and I won't. All I'll ever find is an interpretation of the truth.

Journal clipping, October 1, 1997. I haven't finished my chores. I still want to smoke my pipe for as long as I can. I don't want to think about dying. I could go hide in West Texas. I'd like to, but this isn't a choice—sooner or later, I'd have to die or come back. I could stop everything and settle into being a quiet, puttering old man with no expectations. Would that eliminate fear and revulsion? Hope for moments of de-light? I'll probably keep on keeping on until devastation comes. I don't want to have to think that I have already done all I will do.

Journal clipping, December 2, 1997. How will I ever get everything re-corded, all questions answered? I won't.

Journal clipping, June 25, 1997. I like for my environs to be quiet, calm, stable, perhaps even dull. In here, where I live, it is loud, frenetic, tumultuous, and I can't handle even that. My delusions, at least, have been grand. ¶I imagined that one day I'd be a self, or someone, but somehow I skipped over some phases of development and became a leftover without ever being real. Now, I doubt that there was ever much need. Some think that we've gone too far in our hopes for being individuals. Some think we must "transcend" what they are pleased to call our "radical individualism." Oh, well. Perhaps, all along, I never had a true heart. Surely, at any rate, I was wrong about almost everything. ¶I think it would be sweet, just once in a while, to get everything fixed and settled in my mind. That seldom happens, except in small ways. If I can't get everything right in my mind, perhaps there could be some limit to error and uncertainty, as Peter Meinke's poem "Liquid Paper" suggests:

> If I were God
> I'd authorize Celestial Liquid Paper
> every seven years to whiten our mistakes:
> we should be sorry and live with what we've done
> but seven years is long enough and all of us
> deserve a visit now and then
> to the house where we were born
> before everything got written so far wrong.

But I have been wrong and uncertain about almost everything, including especially myself. ¶I sometimes entertain myself with my own follies. One of these is the hope, largely abandoned in recent years, of searching myself to find the first principles that must surely be buried down in there somewhere. Then, perhaps, I'd find that I am an autonomous and unified soul with some integrity of character. I remember Harold Bloom's admonition in *Omens of Millennium:* "If you seek *yourself* outside yourself, then you will encounter disaster, whether erotic or ideological." I haven't otherwise depended much on philosophers who search for first principles, another clue to my own ignorance, which is sometimes just ignorance, sometimes willful ignorance. At any rate, my faith in philosophers is slight; they seem to want to be exact about inexactness, and to do so in a language that a citizen wouldn't use. They don't talk about people. ¶With or without philosophers, I've had little luck. On those occasions when I decided that I would go hunting for my first principles, I usually followed what I thought might be an appropriate method. If I started with what I seem to believe entirely now, I reasoned, and then asked what I had believed before that enabled me to believe what I seem to believe now and why I believed that, and then asked what I had believed before that and why, then surely I'd get to the sources, the first principles. ¶On one such occasion, I got as far as seven current principles:

1. I believe that if you are the pivot man at second base on a double play, you're supposed to touch second base, not just come close to it.

2. I believe that fresh, strong black coffee is the third greatest material good.

3. I believe that cold white wine, preferably at least somewhat akin to Rhine wine, is the second greatest material good.

4. I believe that coarse-cut burley tobacco with no additives is the greatest material good.

5. I believe that if you are a school teacher, you're supposed to do your homework.

6. I believe that if you are a school teacher, you're supposed to check your zippers and buttons before you go to class.

7. I believe that if you want or need to see something, you have to get in the right place to see it. ¶Here, either my attention waned or my analytical powers fizzled, and I was unable to continue. That has also been true since, and I have come no nearer to those buried first principles, except to learn my limits:

8. I believe that I cannot entirely explain myself to myself. ¶Some things will not be in a scrapbook. I cannot keep, tell, or show them because I have lost them in one or another of the various ways I have been talking about. Others will not be in a scrapbook because I choose not to tell or to show them, though I have kept them. If I could find those first principles, keep, tell, and show them, perhaps I'd be a self, but my identity is blurred around the edges, and in the middle, too.

Though "a label that embraces multitudes," postmodernism is, as Alan Ryan remarks, notable for combining "skepticism about the amount of control that a writer exercises over his or her work" with a "sharp sense of the fragility of personal identity." Ryan continues:

> The idea that each of us is a single Self consorts naturally with the idea that we tell stories, advance theories, and interact with others from one particular viewpoint. Skepticism about such a picture of our identities consorts naturally with the thought that we are at the mercy of the stories we tell, as much as they are at our mercy. It also consorts naturally with an inclination to emphasize just how accidental it is that we hold the views we do, live where we do, and have the loyalties we do.

If I stand against a classroom wall, I tend to disappear. I am mostly sort of beige and grey, as are many institutional walls, and I'm likely to fade into the background of the moment. Perhaps I can argue myself into obsolescence and, with a little help, on into oblivion. I was wrong about much in the past. The present amounts to little. The future is negligible.

Snapshot 15: I have no photograph, and there will be none, of January 29, 1998.

Snapshot 16: I have no photograph, and there will be none, of January 31, 1998.

Snapshot 17: I have no photograph, and there will be none, of February 21, 1998.

I tell about myself. I reference myself. From the start I have done so. I look at myself hoping to see a self. I look at myself hoping to see out of myself. Sometimes what I see is nothing much. What I see is wanting, and insufficiently learned. I look at myself hoping to see out of myself. I cannot see anything well unless I manage to see the veils behind my eyes, and know that I see through both veils and eyes. I cannot at last rid myself of veils and eyes, but I must know that I am already a self looking out of a self. Whenever I see, think, act, speak, or write myself into a rhetoric discernible out there, I am already inside a rhetoric in here. I am always the subject of my own sentences, though I may omit the pronoun. I cannot parse my sentences unless I locate the subject. ¶The other out there is part of our context, or milieu, as David Lowenthal puts it. We are not, however, routinely a part of our own milieu. Whatever self I am that is discernible in my milieu is real. The self in here looking out is real. The two are not identical. I leave to try to become part of my own milieu, and I have to try to learn my own prior rhetoric before I can begin to see the self in here, the self that is seen from out there, and the self out there from the self in here, though I am generally not able to do so. If you and I stand side by side, even hip to haunch, watching what we take to be the same event on Wednesday, March 11, 1998, and if, twenty years from now, or perhaps tomorrow, we are asked to tell what happened, we will not tell the same story, though each of us will tell a true story. Perhaps I will listen to your story and know that you've got it wrong, but I will not easily acknowledge that I, too, have got it wrong. It may even be easy enough for me to see that you are telling an inaccurate story because you are you, telling from a particular vantage point out of your own rhetoric, but it may not be easy, or possible, for me to know that the same is true of my telling, since I will not always, if ever, be able to see myself. But I must try to see what accounts for my personal way of telling the event. ¶I understand that the personal must be in question, given, as they say, the play of the signifier, the indeterminacy of signification, the inaccessibility of Presence. I understand that *personal* derives from *person,* that *person* derives from *persona,* that *persona* means *mask.* I understand that there is no person, if by the word we mean a complete, unitary self confronting a solid, fixed reality, perceiving it directly and accurately, then providing a transcript of a living voice. I understand that personal writing is contaminated by the mistaken claims of autonomous authorship. I understand that no writer writes alone, therefore never just personally; even if he or she is alone in the room, a crowd is there, advising, encouraging, hissing, cursing. ¶When I was a boy in 1936, reaching near the limits of my preschool arithmetic and responding to whatever it is that makes the turn of years and millennia momentarily interesting, I calculated that it was possible for me to live into the twenty-first century. If I could make it, I reckoned, to a fraction past the age of seventy-one, I'd be to the end of 2000, and, another fraction would take me into the new age, if that's what it was going to be. ¶Now, in March, 1998, it still seems possible to get that far, but to expect to last much longer than that scarcely seems feasible or justifiable, if there is any justice. I do not wish to die. I like living most of the time, and I want to smoke my pipe some more, but I have pretty well used up the twentieth century. I have no special need of the twenty-first century, and it will have scant need of me. When the year 2000 ends, I should be over, too. I have achieved the height of mediocrity. I have not been able to keep anyone safe from the cold and dark. I have not created or invented anything either original or worthy. I have, whether in deed or thought, enacted all of my time's favorite sins. ¶I can almost put my fingers on and announce all that the world needs to know for its rescue and salvation. Everything is there in my mind, if I could only understand what I know, or if I could only know what I understand. Everything is there, the debris of generations, if I could only get past the barriers, whether to entry or to exit, of my own mind. I follow what I like to think of as the labyrinthine ways in my mind, only to be startled and shamed by myself, stricken by what I see. Sometimes the labyrinthine paths simply fizzle out, and I don't notice myself at the end. I have done nothing great, notable, or useful. I have not even been able to achieve great sins, though I have regularly performed the trite sins of my time. Trite sins—murder and betrayal, for example— may be huge and monstrous, therefore clearly beyond my reach. They may be small replicas of the huge and monstrous. Then I can manage them and do, routinely. ¶I interrogate myself. Why should I talk about such things? Perhaps I am an exhibitionist. Perhaps I hope to confess, though to whom I do not know, except the world. Perhaps I want to be honest: I did want to gather everything in a scrapbook, though I can't and won't. Perhaps I am trying to understand the rhetorical world I live in beforehand every time I try to say anything. ¶But I can't see the backs of my own eyeballs. I don't know all the early lessons I learned, usually without knowing that I had learned. What I learned from Hopalong Cassidy I have characteristically failed to be and to do. What I learned from the preacher down at the little Baptist church in Jayton I only half learned: I didn't learn religious belief in hope or comfort; I only learned the part about sin and damnation. I don't even know all of my sins, and can't save them, but I am sure about damnation. ¶I don't know that I ever expected to find belief, but I have surely wanted to find comfort. I am sure about damnation. I don't even know all of my sins. Those I am sure about seem sufficient, but I must not name them, though I want to do so.

Journal clipping, June 25, 1997. I have wondered, though not often, how many nice notebooks, journals, logs, records, tablets, and such I have put away or discarded, largely unused because I wanted to start over. I do not seem to have been capable of resisting the compulsion. I am obeying it again. I want to be new. The image of crammed journals, preferably leather bound, has been important in my head at least since I was in my early twenties. It has been a sign of identity and significance. I have achieved neither. I will start again.

Journal clipping, September 24, 1997. I look back to the first entry here, for June 25, 1997. What I said there was all right, accurate enough but insufficient. I have always wanted to be able to start over, but that's not the only reason for scrapping journals and starting new ones. A second, probably more important reason is that in earlier journals I have almost invariably, after bland enough beginnings, started writing down hopes, fantasies, occasional near-truths that then I can't tolerate seeing again or bear to have someone else, by chance, read. I'm doing it again, and if I continue, I'll sooner or later have to destroy this journal, too. I comfort myself with great company for a moment, remembering that Dr. Johnson, late in his life, destroyed some of his own papers. ¶I have wanted to chronicle my sins; I have also wanted to detail every minute of every delight. I have wanted to write everything down, everything, and I have often wondered why that is so. ¶I know some of the reasons. Sometimes, it's a comfort to a fellow to write things down so as to get them out there, at a distance so as to think about them a little more clearly. Some experiences are delightful, joyful, even thrilling; a fellow might consider writing them down so as to revel in them again, though the pleasure would be paler the second or third time around. Some experiences are dreadful, on toward monstrous self-revelations; a fellow might consider writing them down so as to try to face them, though the pain might grow with each encounter. Sometimes a fellow might want to write things down so that they'll be real out there. Sometimes a fellow might want to write things down just to keep them, if not intact, as in a scrapbook. Always, I think, a fellow would want to write things down to praise the particulars of creation, though that doesn't always work. ¶Such reasons, I believe, are good enough and legitimate, but they do not complete the list. I wanted to write a perfect celebration, but of course I cannot, keeping every moment, every detail of my time with the beautiful woman who gave me her energy and spirit, who taught me to see in new ways, who tended me, who fulfilled my hopes and fantasies, and taught me more. I wanted to write a song beyond Solomon's for her and for myself. ¶And I wanted to write everything down, keep all memories, scraps, artifacts, residues, shards, notes, stories, pictures because I am the primary source for the world. ¶I have failed in that too: there is no scrapbook that holds the truth at the end of the world. ¶I might still find some of what I have hunted. Perhaps I have already seen what I was looking for but didn't notice. More likely: what's not here is not out there to be found. Ordinary artifacts that tell the world—the little red race car that had battery-driven headlights—are gone. The Center View Community, the Oriana Community, the old public library, the little house on the Lowrance ranch, my Grandpa's farmhouse and the railroad trestle down below it—all are gone. People are gone, or I haven't found them. Perhaps they have all found untroubled places of rest, but I think that kin and friends and all those others lie in unvisited graves. ¶I guess that I wanted to believe I could compete with hopeless history, catch and keep it all, though there is no scrapbook that holds the truth at the end of the world. ¶And yet stories—histories, that is, and scrapbooks—can hold the blessed, ordinary particulars of creation. No truth waits otherwise. William James says that he "will take a God who lives in the very dirt of private fact—if that would seem a likely place to find him." Yes, let there be stories, histories, pictures that make truth by giving truth a place to be. Truth is always geographically situated, even if we can't find some geographies. Let there be scrapbooks, too, and let them be cluttered. In Jerome Badanes's Holocaust novel, *The Final Opus of Leon Solomon,* Solomon muses:

> I have devoted my life to recovery—a task with grave limitations. It is not possible to fully recover what was lost. The restored collections help give us a certain picture; our scholarship aids us to understand this picture, and serves as a guide. But only the memory holds bits and pieces of what is gone. The memory, however, selects out, just like the doctors in Auschwitz, sentencing some images of the past to the perpetual half-life of sentimentality and official versions, and dooming the remaining (and, I have learned, the more vital) images to immediate oblivion—almost.

A little later, Solomon remarks that images of trivial things "have life-and-death importance, and that is as it should be." But to find what has fallen into oblivion, "you must be aware that this oblivion is always right behind you—and you must often look over your shoulder, suddenly alert for any opportunity to make a lightning raid into its blackness to rescue a single image." ¶I am a scrap. I am made of scraps, loosely basted, holes showing. I have kept some scraps. I have lost more. I have kept some scraps that I cannot show. I cannot show the scraps left over from what has hurt most. I cannot show the scraps left over from what have been my most grievous sins. I cannot show the scraps left over from what has brought the greatest joy and elation.

Videotape 1, never made: A videotape will not catch all that's in a motion beyond all the loveliness and grace of art, when a beautiful woman, in her own will and lust and love, lifted her arms behind her back to loosen her bra for me. ¶I have kept that moment, and others, but will not show it, now or ever. Can't. ¶I look back again to see what is here, to think about what is missing, not shown. I'd like to believe that what I remember and have shown has stayed for good reason. That is probably true. What has stayed is what my mind plays on, plays among, and so it counts, though I have not kept anything whole or remembered anything accurately. What I have forgotten, lost, or not shown also counts. ¶I am the primary source for the world. The world is over when I am over. Leon Solomon muses further:

> A man's private fantasies, which have a rich life of their own, end forever, and as though they never existed, when the man dies—unless he confesses them to another. Or writes them down. If he does write them down, even in a most disguised manner, they become a part—an essential part—of the historical record. With these fantasies recorded, a picture emerges, not of an orderly society of impoverished creatures imprisoned and entertained by a few glittering figures, but of a world where we are all simultaneously kings and lovers, avenging angels and groveling suitors.

I have not confessed, but I am the primary source for the world. The world is over when I am over. Who else will tell what you and I remember and try to make it real but you and me? Who else will show what the world looks like to you and me and try to make it real but you and me? ¶But I have not confessed, have not shown or told all. I am the primary source for the world. The world is over when I am over. My testimony is the only testimony there is for my testimony. I have come to nothing, with my testimony. ¶I have destroyed some evidence of the world. ¶I have allowed some evidence of the world to be lost. ¶I have withheld some evidence of the world. ¶Only scraps remain. ¶I wanted to bring back, to hold, ordinary artifacts, places, events, people, to bring them all back, to keep them, though they are dead or gone or missing, or dead and gone and missing. Only scraps remain. ¶I go back to Augustine. "I have become," he says, "a problem to myself, like land which a farmer works only with difficulty and at the cost of much sweat." I cannot claim that I was once exuberant, though there have been remarkable moments. I cannot claim that now my soul is sick, with no interest in life. Both exuberance and soul-sickness are far too extreme for a fellow who has spent most of his life sort of in the middle. There in the middle, or on the darker edge of the middle, a dreary paleness seems to offer few glimmers of hope and anticipation; life is, if not without interest, less interesting, and it is easy to spend it counting regrets: I have destroyed some evidence of the world; I have allowed some evidence of the world to be lost; I have withheld some evidence of the world. I list regrets, count them, pore over them. I compose a litany of regrets. I regret what I have lost or withheld. I regret that I have shown inadequately what I have shown. ¶And then, at last, I remember that I am puzzled by my own regrets, curious about them. One way to deal with dreary paleness, bleakness, is to go into it and to see if you come out on the other side. I am curious. I investigate myself. Why such regrets? ¶If I don't search for the once-familiar evidences of our ordinary lives, then they will be gone. If I don't get them out and study them, they will be gone. If I don't try to understand them and myself, we'll be gone. We can only learn to understand mystery by studying the ordinary evidences of our lives, the site of mystery. ¶I don't want an all-new life. I do not wish to be born again. Curiosity and puzzlement about this one, I think, will suffice. A life may enable us to compose a new life, though we sometimes spend eons reiterating the same life. If we do manage to come into a new life, we may find capacities that we didn't own before, new revelations of ourselves and of our cultures, but entering a new life doesn't release us into unbound vision or show us unfettered truth. ¶The light from the desk lamp on the table where I work catches in the heavy plastic frames of my glasses. I see what is before me, framed by that reflected light, as well as can be reasonably expected, but if I look up and out of the window, then I cannot see what is before me out yonder. I change glasses and see out there, but now I can no longer see what is before me here. When we make a new life, or stumble into a new life, we do so through the instrumentality of the old life. I find my far-seeing glasses by looking through my near-seeing glasses. I put on a new life and take up its instrumentalities. Then it's difficult to see the old life, or to find my other glasses. I do so eventually, looking, hunting, fumbling. ¶Curiosity and puzzlement—that is to say, a need to see—will suffice. A new life rises in an old life if is stoked by curiosity and puzzlement. Then, perhaps, we can see better by the new light. We walk by burning bushes every day, but fail to notice. We walk in magnificence every day, but do not notice. Sometimes, especially blessed, we lie down in magnificence, but do not remark it. ¶Grandma—my father's mother—saved scraps. Then she made quilts. When I was a boy, I sometimes watched her, though I didn't always understand what I was seeing. Grandma wasn't a very good cook. She wasn't cuddly. Sometimes she was mean-tempered: the world didn't always suit her well. She was illiterate. Her eyes were a little crossed, and her vision was poor, except up close. When she was fifty-eight, my Grandpa died. She had nothing. She lived for another twenty years, first with one of her children, then with another, in a rotation I never understood. She was lost. But she collected rags, scraps from other people's sewing projects, pieces of worn-out shirts and whatever. Then, after a while, she made quilts. I remember watching her, but until just now I had not taken pains to notice the significance of one step in her method. ¶As she collected scraps, she sorted them by some standard I was never able to understand and tied them in little bundles. When more scraps accumulated, she would untie her bundles and go through the sorting process, adding the new scraps. In time, when enough scraps had accumulated, she made a quilt. I never saw her lay out all the scraps to consider them all at once. She had no printed pattern or design. The design, I guess, was in her head. She began with a single scrap. She cut it to suit her purpose, then took another scrap and cut it. In time, she changed the shape she was cutting, and by and by began to stack like shapes together. Within a day or so, then, she would sew the shapes together to make the first square of the quilt. Until just now, I had not paid sufficient attention to the cutting. None of her scraps survived entire, though she wasted little. When she cut her scraps to make her shapes, she left something out. I'm glad I noticed or remembered that. ¶I guess we never keep our scraps entire. Her quilts were beautiful. After a while, each of her grandchildren came to own one. We enjoyed them. Mine was lovely, made to a design that no one else had ever seen before she made her quilt. ¶I think, too, that each of us has seen what no one else has ever seen. Each of us is the last of some tribe, the last teller of the last story, the last keeper of the last scrapbook, the last sewer of the last quilt.

This book is a joint venture of
the Missouri State University Departments of
English and Art and Design.
With series lists in "Arts and Letters" and
"Ozarks History and Culture,"
Moon City Press books feature collaborations
between MSU students and faculty
over the various aspects of publication—
research, writing, editing, layout and design.
This book was co-edited by James S. Baumlin,
MSU Professor of English,
and Eric Knickerbocker,
an undergraduate Philosophy major.